MODERN POETRY

MODERN POETRY

A PERSONAL ESSAY

BY

LOUIS MACNEICE

SECOND EDITION

WITH AN INTRODUCTION BY

WALTER ALLEN

OXFORD
AT THE CLARENDON PRESS
1968

Oxford University Press, Ely House, London W. 1

GLASGOW NEW YORK TORONTO MELBOURNE WELLINGTON
CAPE TOWN SALISBURY IBADAN NAIROBI LUSAKA ADDIS ABABA
BOMBAY CALCUTTA MADRAS KARACHI LAHORE DACCA
KUALA LUMPUR HONG KONG TOKYO

FIRST EDITION 1938
SECOND EDITION 1968

PRINTED IN GREAT BRITAIN

INTRODUCTION

When *Modern Poetry* was first published in 1938 it had all the appearance of a manifesto, even of propaganda. MacNeice, aged thirty, a member of a generation of poets significantly different from that which had preceded it, was arguing the case particularly for the poetry of his friends Auden and Spender, which was a socially committed poetry; and in the process found himself analysing the nature of poetry and surveying its course until his own day. Thirty years later, the poetic scene is plainly very different from what it was when MacNeice was writing; the predictions implicit in the book have been fulfilled, if at all, only to a limited degree; and since 1938 there have been more than one kind of reaction, both in Britain and in the United States, against the sort of poetry MacNeice was advocating. On the face of it, much of his thesis has been disproved by history. Auden himself, who still seems the archetypal poet of the thirties in England and who is in a sense the hero of MacNeice's book, has not only repudiated the notion, fundamental to the book, that poets should be socially committed but has also repudiated a fair number of poems he wrote during the period and that seem still among its most characteristic.

One would expect *Modern Poetry*, then, to have dated. It is, after all, a common fate of manifestos for schools or movements of poetry to end up having

curiosity value only. Yet this has not been the fate
of MacNeice's book, manifesto though in part it is.
Indeed, its interest and importance today seem to
me much greater than one would have prophesied
for it when it first appeared. And the interest and
importance are twofold. One is historical—and here
it is relevant to remember that the book was published just as MacNeice was reaching the half-way
point in the writing of his long poem *Autumn
Journal*, which, like *Modern Poetry*, is a key-document of its period and will remain so, it seems to me
as certain as anything can be, for as long as men and
women are interested in the period. If anyone wishes
to know what it was like to be young, intelligent,
sensitive—a poet—living in London during the last
grim months of 1938, when the gas-masks were
being distributed and the trenches dug in the parks,
with Mr. Chamberlain flying back from Berchtes-
gaden with peace in our time and the Spanish Civil
War dragging itself out to another fascist victory,
more than anything else I know in prose or verse
Autumn Journal is the book to read: just as *Modern
Poetry* is the book to read if you wish to know how
the poets who seem now most characteristic of their
generation felt about their craft and their responsi-
bility as poets.

In *Modern Poetry* MacNeice became the spokesman of a generation of poets, and, with the benefit
of hindsight, it is not difficult to see how this came
about. *Modern Poetry* and *Autumn Journal*, the prose
work and the poem, must have been expressions of
one single impulse; *Modern Poetry* provides the

critical rationale of the poem. In a sense, MacNeice was justifying not only Auden's and Spender's poetry particularly but also the poem he himself was about to write. This was not apparent at the time; it couldn't be, because *Autumn Journal* was not published until a year later: and at the time of its appearance, *Modern Poetry* was not at all an obvious book for MacNeice to write, as, for instance, *A Hope for Poetry* seemed an obvious book to come from Day Lewis. MacNeice today is thought of as quintessentially a thirties poet, as one of the four legs of Roy Campbell's monster MacSpaunday, the others being Auden, Spender, and Day Lewis. But MacSpaunday was a later invention, and during the thirties themselves MacNeice did not appear at all a typical figure. The poetic trinity was Auden, Spender, and Day Lewis, whose names went together as trippingly on the tongue as those of Freeman, Hardy, and Willis. It was these who were the socially committed poets calling, in their different ways, for 'new styles of architecture, a change of heart', in Auden's words, celebrating the future, as Spender did, in such lines as

> Death is another milestone on their way,
> With laughter on their lips and with winds blowing
>   round them
> They speak simply
> Of how this one excelled all others in making
>   driving belts,

demanding revolution in the state as well as in poetry.

In this context, despite his close friendship with

Auden, with whom he had collaborated in *Letters from Iceland*, MacNeice seemed a curiously aloof figure, something of an odd man out. The mood was Left, indeed Marxist and, in the case of Day Lewis at least, paid-up Communist: MacNeice was Left in a general way but he was certainly anything but a Communist. What was immediately obvious in his verse, in contrast with the committed exuberance of Auden and Day Lewis and the fervour of Spender, were doubts and reservations. When one read his poem, 'The Individualist Speaks', with its last line, 'But I will escape, with my dog, to the far side of the Fair', it was difficult not to read into it a repudiation of all mass movements whether of the Left or of the Right.

The poetry MacNeice wrote in the thirties was not only more sceptical than that of the contemporaries with whom he is now generally coupled, it was also more personal, and of the elements that go into its making two in particular seem worth isolating here. One is his identification with the lives not of 'The Workers' but of what, for want of a better word, one can only call ordinary people or perhaps suburban man. It was not, of course, anything like complete identification: aloofness was part of MacNeice's nature; but it did imply that he recognized that what he had in common with them was greater and more important than the differences. This recognition came to him with all the force of revelation. It was tied up with his going to live in Birmingham, where he went straight from undergraduate life at Oxford to teach in the University. It would scarcely be possible to exaggerate the effect of Birmingham, the great black sprawling industrial city, upon him. The evidence is in his poems and also, explicitly, in the long fragment of autobiography, *The Strings are False*, which is a speaking likeness of the man. He went to Birmingham an aesthete and in some respects remained an aesthete all his life; but in Birmingham he discovered common humanity and recognized it in himself.

The other element I want to single out from his thirties poems is the sense of foreboding, of impending doom for himself and for people like him. It is the note struck in the poem 'Turf-Stacks'. It receives striking expression in what seems to me the finest, most masterly, of his early poems, 'An Eclogue for Christmas', in which the aesthete and townee, who was MacNeice, debates with the countryman and man of the open air who was also MacNeice:

> We shall go down like Paleolithic Man
> Before some new Ice Age or Genghis Khan.

And if it is argued that this is an early poem, one can only say that the feeling behind it is echoed some years later in the poem addressed to Auden in *Letters from Iceland*.

This sense of foreboding, of impending doom—or rather, MacNeice's way of reacting to it, since the mood itself was common to the thirties poets—was what at the time differentiated MacNeice from the committed poets. They were, if not optimistic, certainly militant. The early poems of Auden, for instance, are exhortations, calls to action. By contrast, MacNeice is doubtful and pessimistic.

Was *Modern Poetry*, then, an expression of a sudden conversion to commitment? It seems to me true that in it MacNeice lines himself up, as it were, with Auden and Spender and the other poets of Michael Roberts's anthology *New Signatures* (to which he himself did not contribute) in a way that must suggest to a reader ignorant of his poetry that he had much more in common with them, where belief in political action is concerned, than he actually had. But there are other factors that have to be taken into account, of which the most obvious is the Spanish Civil War. This, together with what it plainly portended for Europe, was one of those events that force men to take sides, to stand up and be counted, as we say, regardless of whether they are politically minded by temperament or not. MacNeice's attitude towards the Spanish Civil War was unambiguous. Commitment was forced upon him and accepted.

But that *Modern Poetry* may well have been in part the expression of a moment of conversion to positive commitment is not nearly so important or so interesting as the fact that it throws invaluable light on MacNeice himself, the poet he was and the kind of poetry he wrote all his life. So the book is not only a key-document to a period in poetry, it is also a key-document for all who are interested in MacNeice's poetry. Seen from this point of view, we can watch MacNeice using the poetry of Auden and

Spender in particular to justify his own, both what he had already written and what he was still to write. I have said that MacNeice is generally thought of today as quintessentially a thirties poet. This seems to me to be just. Indeed, it could be argued that he alone remained faithful throughout his life to the conception of poetry we mean when we talk of English thirties poetry. He did not have to repudiate his early work as Auden has felt it necessary to repudiate so much of his. He underwent no religious conversion; there are no dramatic changes in the nature of his poetry or in the preoccupations that inform it, as again there have been in Auden's and also Day Lewis's. There is no obvious development in his poetry. The verses in his second volume, *Poems*, which made his reputation, are as good as anything he ever wrote. What he did in the thirty years that followed was to go on writing poems that were often as good but were scarcely different in kind. The poet of the magnificent posthumous book, *The Burning Perch*, is immediately recognizable as the poet of *Poems*; and already, in that early volume, he was the master of his medium and, I believe, a totally original poet.

And the thirties was the right period for him to have emerged in, and better than anyone else he seems to me to sum up its poetic virtues. In so far as it can be seen as a self-contained period—and in poetry it was more self-contained than decades normally are—it was characterized by a strong reaction against symbolism, against private poetry or learned poetry, in opposition to which it set up the notion of public poetry, public in the sense that ideally it could be accessible to all men and women of good will. It could be topical, light, slangy, its imagery derived as required from the furnishings of the world of common men. The word 'journalistic' suddenly took on connotations of praise as applied to poetry. Admittedly, the poets of the decade often fell far short in practice of their ambitions in these respects, but they were more successful, it seems to me, than they were given credit for. Today, we find their aims embodied in the poetry, for instance, of Philip Larkin and Kingsley Amis; and to turn to much more popular poets, you can spot the influence of Auden especially in some of the lyrics of the Beatles. They were attempting, in fact, the kind of poetry J. M. Synge had in mind when he wrote:

I have often thought that at the side of poetic diction, which everyone condemns, modern verse uses a great deal of poetic material, using poetic in the same special sense. The poetry of exaltation will always be the highest, but when men lose their poetic feeling for ordinary life, and cannot write poetry of ordinary things, their exalted poetry is likely to lose its strength of exaltation, in the way men cease to build beautiful churches when they have lost happiness in building shops. Many of the older poets, such as Villon and Herrick and Burns, used the whole of their personal life as their material, and the verse written in this way was read by strong men, and thieves, and deacons, not by little cliques alone.

MacNeice does not quote from that passage of Synge in *Modern Poetry* but he does, in his first chapter, quote some further sentences from the same essay:

In these days poetry is usually a flower of evil or good; but it is the timber of poetry that wears most surely, and there is no timber that has not strong roots among the clay and worms. . . . Even if we grant that exalted poetry can be kept successful by itself, the strong things of life are needed in poetry also, to show that what is exalted or tender is not made by feeble blood. It may almost be said that before verse can be human again it must learn to be brutal.

This notion of Synge's of the wholeness, the total comprehensiveness, of poetry runs through Mac-Neice's book. It is the standard by which he judges poetry both of the past and of the present; and in his last chapter he produces a paraphrase of Synge in terms of himself:

My own prejudice, therefore, is in favour of poets whose worlds are not too esoteric. I would have a poet able-bodied, fond of talking, a reader of the newspapers, capable of pity and laughter, informed in economics, appreciative of women, involved in personal relationships, actively interested in politics, susceptible to physical impressions. The relationship between life and literature is almost impossible to analyse, but it should not be degraded into something like the translation of one language into another. For life is not literary, while literature is not, in spite of Plato, essentially second hand.

It would be easy to draw up a long list of poets, among them some of the greatest, though they would not include Homer, Chaucer, and Shakespeare, who would not at all satisfy MacNeice's own prejudice; but the real point is that, when all allowances have been made for the especial circumstances of the time at which it was written, it remains

a very adequate description of MacNeice himself as
man and poet and very well indicates the kind of life,
the world if you like, to be found in his verse. His
was not the poetry of exaltation, anything but. It was
often a pyrotechnic display of hard, bright, dazzling
images—not for nothing he called his first book of
verse *Blind Fireworks*—of unexpected rhymes un-
expectedly placed; it contains echoes of nursery
rhymes and jazz songs and takes in slang and
clichés—in homage to which he wrote a memorable
poem. It is often highly topical. But the words
always dance to MacNeice's own individual tune,
and the result is a strongly idiosyncratic poetry
which is the vehicle of strongly idiosyncratic comment, allied often to the essay or even to the newspaper columnist's article—and also, and I think
increasingly over the years, to the poetry of Horace,
whose name crops up so often in this book and
whom MacNeice translated so beautifully.

It is from its nature public poetry, and it was
absolutely logical for MacNeice to have used poetry
as what might be called an applied art for so many
years in the service of the B.B.C.; but it is also the
poetry of a whole man, and everything that happened
to the man went to feed it. It was the product too
of the poet's sympathy and identification with the
ordinary aspects of mankind. This identification is
made crystal-clear in the very first paragraph of the
book:

The poet is primarily a spokesman, making statements or
incantations on behalf of himself or others—usually for both,
for it is difficult to speak for oneself without speaking for

others or to speak for others without speaking for oneself. The poet, therefore, in a sense is man at his most self-conscious, but this means consciousness of himself as man, not consciousness of himself as poet.

He goes on:

Poets for more than a hundred years now have been suffering from the latter kind of self-consciousness. They have felt that their expressed attitude to the world must be peculiarly the attitude of *poets*, that therefore much of the world was unfit subject for poetry because it was itself un-poetic.

He traces the history of this divorce between the poet and other men and its consequences for poetry, and it is by the appeal to the identification of poet with common man that he criticizes older poets of his own time whom he greatly admires, such as Yeats and Eliot. Much of what he has to say is, of course, property common to himself and the poets who were his friends. One recalls that Auden in his introduction to *The Poet's Tongue*, an anthology for boys he compiled with John Garrett—MacNeice, admitting that it would give boys a 'more catholic conception of poetry' than was to be found in Pal-grave, criticizes it for containing 'too high a per-centage of light verse, comic verse, nonsense, and doggerel'—defined poetry as 'memorable speech', and much of what MacNeice says is a prose version of passages in Auden's 'Letter to Lord Byron'. This is not to suggest at all that MacNeice was writing under Auden's influence. He was no doubt heartened by the examples of Auden's verse that supported his own case; but he was always uncompromisingly his own man and *Modern Poetry* is his own book.

It is, in fact, as idiosyncratic as his poetry. It is characteristic of him not only that he should use samples of his own verse as texts to illustrate critical points but that, to demonstrate that 'the poet is a specialist in something which everyone practises', he should do so by describing his own development as a poet and a reader of poetry. Though, as he says more than once in his book, he could see no absolute distinction between poetry and prose, it has always seemed to me that MacNeice in practice tended to be impatient of prose. I suspect that, as a medium, he found it too slow and ponderous. When he turned to prose it was almost invariably for autobiographical purposes. Certainly everything he wrote in prose is strongly autobiographical, overtly so in *The Strings are False* but almost as much in *Modern Poetry* and in the Clark Lectures on allegory he gave at Cambridge towards the end of his life. He is himself, as it were, his final court of appeal.

It is this personal quality that gives *Modern Poetry* the freshness which it still has after thirty years and will have, I believe, for a long time to come. It is a poet's book about poetry, not an academic's or a critic's. MacNeice indeed was generally sceptical of formal criticism. As he says in the first paragraph of his final chapter,

Writing about poetry often becomes a parlour game. The critic is more interested in producing a water-tight system of criticism than in the objects which are his data. I have written this book as one who enjoys reading and writing certain (probably limited) kinds of poetry and is only concerned with criticism in so far as it clears away misapprehensions and opens the gate to poetry itself.

For MacNeice, the objects which are his data are all-important, and it is out of them that his criticism springs. In this he is in the line of those English poets from Ben Jonson to Eliot and Robert Graves whom we also remember as critics. The mark of them all is a distrust of general theories of poetry that do not chime with their own experience as makers of poetry. What they all do is to remake the idea of poetry in their own image, or in the image of the kind of poetry they themselves are concerned to write; and this is substantially what MacNeice does in *Modern Poetry*.

Whether, at the end of his life, MacNeice would still have stood by everything he wrote in his book we cannot know. It is, after all, a young man's book. It has its brashnesses; and there are moments, it seems to me, especially in writing about his immediate contemporaries and friends, when he construes promise as positive achievement. And some of the predictions for poetry implicit in the book have been contradicted by what actually happened in the years that followed its publication. Yet even as a work of formal criticism—and as such it is most easily assailable—it remains for me an impressive book. It is much more than a work of propaganda for the 'new' poetry of a specific decade: it re-states in contemporary terms the case for a kind of poetry we ignore at our peril, that poetry which may be called heightened conversation, the kind of poetry that we associate with Horace and with Pope and Dryden, and in our time with Auden, particularly in his later manifestations, and perhaps most conspicuously with MacNeice himself. It is full of brilliant *aperçus* which remind us that its author was a man who brought to the study of poetry and the writing of it extensive reading in several literatures ancient and modern. There is, for instance, the remark, when MacNeice is writing of his growing appreciation of poetry at Marlborough: 'Homer gave me an example of verse-writing which was homogeneous but yet elastic enough to represent much of life's variety. I have noticed since that many modern theories of poetry could not make room for Homer.' The comment is a reminder that, however novel MacNeice's theory and practice may have seemed thirty years ago, they were based on the oldest poetic tradition.

Again, as an example of the unblinkered perception, the ability to see things new, that runs through the book, I'd instance the passage in the chapter on imagery in which MacNeice discusses the Metaphysical poets and Dr. Johnson's reaction to them:

Dryden and Pope contented themselves with the more conventional classic metaphors and similes, for clarity's sake dropping both the subtle algebra of the metaphysicals and the word-auras of Shakespeare. But Dr. Johnson in turning his back on the Metaphysical Poets also looks forward to the Romantic Revival: 'Their attempts were always analytick; they broke every image into fragments: and could no more

represent, by their slender conceits and laboured particularities, the prospects of nature, or the scenes of life, than he
who dissects a sunbeam with a prism can exhibit the *wide
effulgence* of a summer morn [italics mine].' The poet's
object, this passage at least implies, is to give a general impression roughly appropriate to his subject-matter rather than
any clean-cut formula.

This shrewd comment on Johnson, running as it does
contrary to conventional interpretations of him,
seems to me literary criticism of a high order.

Then there is the manner of the book. There is
a complete absence of critical jargon and affectations,
as there is also of belletrism. The manner is that of
conversation, but the tone is rapid, urgent, even
impatient at times, as of a man who is totally committed to the importance of what he is saying, a poet
for whom the writing of poetry and therefore the
thinking about it really do come as naturally as
leaves to a tree. Which brings us back to what is its
final importance and interest: the light it throws on
MacNeice himself.

WALTER ALLEN

PREFACE

THIS book is a plea for *impure* poetry, that is, for poetry conditioned by the poet's life and the world around him.

I have not attempted here to give a full survey of contemporary poetry. There are many poets, and a few good poets, whom I have not mentioned. I am putting a personal point of view, but one with which, I feel, many readers of poetry will sympathize.

The poet, I consider, is both critic and entertainer (and his criticism will cut no ice unless he entertains). Poetry to-day should steer a middle course between pure entertainment ('escape poetry') and propaganda. Propaganda, the extreme development of 'critical' poetry, is also the defeat of criticism. And the mere slogan-poet contradicts his name—*poiētes*, a 'maker'. The poet is a maker, not a retail trader. The writer to-day should be not so much the mouthpiece of a community (for then he will only tell it what it knows already) as its conscience, its critical faculty, its generous instinct. In a world intransigent and over-specialized, falsified by practical necessities, the poet must maintain his elasticity and refuse to tell lies to order. Others can tell lies more efficiently; no one except the poet can give us poetic truth.

L. M.

CONTENTS

I. A CHANGE OF ATTITUDE . . 1

II. MY CASE-BOOK: CHILDHOOD . . 31

III. MY CASE-BOOK: PUBLIC SCHOOL . 47

IV. MY CASE-BOOK: OXFORD . . 62

V. THE PERSONAL FACTOR . . . 75

VI. IMAGERY 90

VII. RHYTHM AND RHYME . . . 114

VIII. DICTION 136

IX. OBSCURITY 154

X. LIGHTER POETRY AND DRAMA . . 178

XI. CONCLUSION 197

I

A CHANGE OF ATTITUDE

THE poet is primarily a spokesman, making statements or incantations on behalf of himself or others—usually for both, for it is difficult to speak for oneself without speaking for others or to speak for others without speaking for oneself. The poet, therefore, in a sense is man at his most self-conscious, but this means consciousness of himself as man, not consciousness of himself as poet. Poets for more than a hundred years now have been suffering from the latter kind of self-consciousness. They have felt that their expressed attitude to the world must be peculiarly the attitude of *poets*, that therefore much of the world was unfit subject for poetry because it was itself unpoetic.

The divorce between the poet and other men or between the poet and himself as a man has been correlated by Marxist critics with the rigid differentiation both of classes and functions in a capitalist society. Thus the Greek poet of the fifth century B.C. wrote his poems as a member of a city-state, a member who took as much part as most people in the activities of the community and who shared with that community a certain morality, a certain number of social and aesthetic preferences, a nucleus of religious belief. His attitude as poet was not distinguished from his attitude as man, which naturally resulted in much of his

poetry being didactic or moralizing. A Greek poet
could write:

> ὑγιαίνειν μὲν ἄριστον ἀνδρὶ θνατῷ,
> δεύτερον δὲ φυὰν καλὸν γενέσθαι,
> τὸ τρίτον δὲ πλουτεῖν ἀδόλως,
> καὶ τὸ τέταρτον ἡβᾶν μετὰ τῶν φίλων.

'The best thing for a mortal man is to be healthy;
the second to possess a fine physique (?); the third
to be wealthy with integrity; the fourth to enjoy
one's prime among friends.'

Other Greeks would have certainly disputed this
ranking, but none would have denied that it is part
of a poet's legitimate business to say what he thinks
are the best or the next best goods for man, or, in
Matthew Arnold's words, to criticize life. It was
assumed that life was the source and subject of
poetry. And life for the Greeks meant life within a
community.

The modern poet, on the other hand, is often both
a 'rebel' against and a parasite upon his community.
He makes it his pride to have different values and
beliefs from those of the community, while at the
same time he demands that the community shall support him and his poetry for their own sake in the
same way that an appreciative oyster might support
the pearl that grows in it. The poet seems no longer
organic to the community.

For this reason poets and artists developed the
doctrine of Art for Art's Sake. The community did
not appear to need them, so, tit for tat, they did not
need the community. This being granted, it was no

longer necessary or even desirable to make one's poetry either intelligible or sympathetic to the community. Further, it was no longer desirable to let the community intrude into the subject of one's work; if it was never going to call, one need not hang out its photograph. But the trouble with words is that every word is a community-product. The poets, however, did the best they could. Ignoring the fact that all words are products of human life but recognizing the fact that human life is essentially life within communities, they set out to exclude as much as possible of this life from their poetry, hoping that the words remaining would not betray their origin. Parnassianism and Symbolism in France, the poetry of the nineties in England, and, later, Imagism in America, were all attempts to divorce art from life—unsuccessful attempts because their poems still represented life, but successful in so far as this life was whittled away to a shadow of a portion of itself—the make-believe life of aesthetes, the life of dreams, a life divorced from morals or the reason or community values, a parasite, a luxury. This was a logical process, for the poet was already a luxury himself.

Poets to-day are working back from luxury-writing and trying once more to become functional. Luxury-writing was the logical development of the Romantic Revival. And yet, paradoxically, the poets of the Romantic Revival thought of themselves as functional—as prophets, preachers, unacknowledged legislators. But as they preached or prophesied from an anarchist position their message failed to fuse with their poetry and we are left with messages on the one hand and (usually) fantasy on the other (witness that very unsatisfactory work, *Prometheus Unbound*). These poets and their successors, the great Victorians, surveyed a large field, but always from the royal box or the high priest's chair. Their public view was inadequate because they always felt themselves so vastly superior to the public. Consequently their best poetry is their private poetry, e.g. the early lyrics of Tennyson. The moral poetry of Tennyson is thin and shoddy, like a mass-produced article, when compared even with Pope's *An Essay on Man*, let alone with Milton.

It was by reaction from this poetry, which they felt to be priggish or pontifical or merely dull and over-padded, that poets towards the end of the nineteenth century jettisoned moral values and the ordinary concerns of humanity. They decided, after reading Tennyson or Browning, that morality and humanity were impurities in poetry instead of seeing that the impurity lay in the poet's attitude rather than in his subject-matter. An impure piece of moralizing is often more tiresome than an impure piece of word-painting, but that does not mean that word-painting is a purer business for the writer than moralizing. Art for Art's Sake was a doctrine of cowardice. Poets were afraid they might be thought prigs or bores.

When a poet becomes preoccupied with looking for the essentials of poetry he is lost. Good poets have written in order to describe something or to preach something—with their eye on the object or the end. The essence of the poetry does not lie in the thing described or in the message imparted but in the resulting concrete unity, the poem. But no one can set out to write poetry by merely attempting to bottle the essence of it—just as no one can win a race by standing, to start with, at the tape.

Words are essentially a vehicle of communication and so *ipso facto* have intellectual, emotional, or moral connotations. The aesthete in words by trying to whittle them down into something less defeats himself. So Matthew Arnold was right in insisting on 'the all-importance of the choice of a subject; the necessity of accurate construction; and the subordinate character of expression', and Walter Pater was wrong in attaching primary importance to 'style'. For the poet's first business is *mentioning* things. Whatever musical or other harmonies he may incidentally evoke, the fact will remain that such and such things—and not others—have been mentioned in his poem. Selection of material is of primary importance (on analysis even this selection will be found to come under the question of Form), and the poet should select material which vitally interests him personally rather than material which is fashionable. If, however, he is a fairly normal person (and it is desirable that poets should be neither half-wits nor out-and-out mystics nor any kind of extraordinary pervert) the result should not be esoteric.

All the material of life is material for poetry, but many of those who have proclaimed this—for example, the Imagists—have drawn exactly the wrong conclusion from it—namely, that anything will do to write a poem about because it is the poem and not the thing which matters; in so thinking they belittle the poem itself, for they are really saying that it is style which matters and not content. [Compare the 'Pure Form' school of painting.] And they are not only belittling the poem, they are belittling their precious concept, 'style'. For style without content is bad style.

I would say that the poet may write about anything provided that that thing matters to him to start with, for then it will bring with it into the poem the intellectual or emotional or moral significance which it has for him in life. And without such significance a poem has no backbone. Those who say that such significance is irrelevant to poetry have merely to look, for refutation, at a number of accepted great lines:

> In la sua voluntade é nostra pace

or

> Τὸ κάλλος αὐτῆς τὸν βίον διώλεσεν

or

> The expense of spirit in a waste of shame
> Is lust in action.

On their theory these lines would be bad poetry unless they argue that their value lies purely in their shape or music, in which case I should say, 'Tell me another.'

When the English poets of the *fin de siècle* jettisoned from poetry the impurities of the Mid-Victorians, what remained? *An Anthology of 'Nineties' Verse* (edited by A. J. Symonds) contains the following typical titles: The Three Musicians, The Masquerade, Plainte Eternelle, The Memphian Temple,

Vesperal, La Gioconda, Les Demoiselles de Sauve, Nihilism, Beauty Accurst [notice the spelling], Sea-Shell Murmurs, White Dreaming, In the Key of Blue, The Absinthe-Drinker, Maquillage, The Harlot's House, Odour, He Remembers Forgotten Beauty. This ninetyish aestheticism is an example of what we should now call 'escapism'—a term used over-glibly. In a sense all art is an escape like a boat in which we ride over life. But the real escapist is the man who sits in his boat while keeping it moored to the bank. The escapist turns to art to forget life, not to be able to face it more securely. Obviously all practice of art helps one in a sense to forget life and is therefore an escape, but there is a distinction between the escape of a man who, having been in a war, writes either honest descriptions of war ('to get it off his chest') or honest descriptions of anything he meets with in the light of his own experience, which inevitably includes that war, and the man who, having been in a war, resorts to describing dreams which he has never met with and which imply the non-existence of wars.

All poetry probably contains an element of wish-fulfilment and a certain recognition of hard facts, but they are obviously found in poets mixed in very different proportions. The distinction between escapist art and art which is a 'criticism of life' is a difference of degree. Theocritus is more escapist than Euripides, Spenser than Chaucer, Livy than Thucydides, the Seicentist poets than Dante, Keats than Shakespeare, Mallarmé than Baudelaire. The nineties poets did to some extent criticize life, but their own lives were both limited and artificial, and that small portion of them which, on a strict aesthetic censorship, they admitted into their poetry was still more so.

This limitation of subject-matter inevitably affected their form. Their writing was pretty or languid—drawling alexandrines, petite stanzas.

'You in your small corner and I in mine' was their principle and the corners were tastefully fitted up. But they forgot that a corner is by rights the corner of a room.

These nineties aesthetes were followed by other poets whose superficial reaction from them concealed an essential similarity. The Georgians with their enthusiasm for simplicity, health, nature, instead of for rouge, decadence, suicide, were still just as much in a corner, just as present-day teashops are equally unnatural whether they are 'Moorish' or 'Tudor'.

The Georgians, in opposition to the aesthetes, professed to bring back happiness into poetry, but their happiness rings no more true than the fastidious gloom of their predecessors. Thus they idyllized the country-side without being rooted, as nature-poets should be, in their subject (I except a few poets such as Edward Thomas). They are mainly townsmen on excursion. Sometimes they cover up their lyrical eulogies with whimsicality, as Rupert Brooke did in writing about Grantchester. With their narrowness of range and frequent woolliness of thought went an insipid technique. The versification is facile to match the lack of tension in the thought.

Apart from idyllizing the English country-side, the

Georgians also took emotional trips to the Orient or to childhood. There is comparatively little Georgian poetry which reveals any consciousness of modern London or the large provincial cities; the Industrial Revolution might never have happened. They were rightly determined to be less 'literary' than their predecessors but, dropping literature, they had not the strength to take up life. They failed to realize the demands of J. M. Synge (1908):

> In these days poetry is usually a flower of evil or good; but it is the timber of poetry that wears most surely, and there is no timber that has not strong roots among the clay and worms. . . . Even if we grant that exalted poetry can be kept successful by itself, the strong things of life are needed in poetry also, to show that what is exalted or tender is not made by feeble blood. It may almost be said that before verse can be human again it must learn to be brutal.

In America, contemporary with the Georgians, the Imagists were following a similar, if a more pretentious, line. An organized group, they even issued a manifesto (1913) which contained, among others, the following professions:

> To allow absolute freedom in the choice of subject. [It is implied that it makes no odds *what* the subject is.]

> To present an image . . . we believe that poetry should render particulars exactly and not deal with vague generalities. [But why must a generality be vague? What about mathematics? A poet in a sense always generalizes; here I agree with Aristotle. The camera can give you my face at this particular moment with a particular fly walking on it at a particular point, but I can never give you that in words.]

> To produce poetry that is hard and clear, never blurred or indefinite. [This is in conscious reaction from the French

Symbolists, but the Imagists' images in a vacuum seem no more concrete than the Symbolists' floating suggestions.]

A few poets, from the nineties to the War, stand as individuals outside this torpid procession. Thus Yeats, the poet who professionally 'Remembers Forgotten Beauty', worked through the ancient Irish legends and modern Irish folk-lore and eventually, though identifying himself with the Irish nationalist movement, had to recognize the palpable realities of living people and contemporary problems. His verse, correspondingly toughened, became sharper and more nervous.

Housman and Kipling went their own ways, Kipling having the courage of his vulgarity and Housman, a born don, writing of love and heroics. Housman's field was narrow and a mock-pastoral field at that, but his verse, being stiffened with irony and wit and memorable from its music, was at least 'critical' poetry in Arnold's sense though the criticism was neither wide nor deep. His hanged man, his soldiers, are over-picturesque, but carry more emotion and more meaning than the suicidal languors, say, of Dowson. Housman's neat little hymn-tune patterns—an unconscious irony of technique—enhance the irony of his attitude.

The brutality and humanity demanded by Synge both came into poetry at once—with the War. The War blew the back out of the Georgian corner. Wilfred Owen, who would otherwise have written aesthete's verse in the Keats tradition, was enabled to write instead about living Man or men under conditions which made real his own communion with them. But when the War was over and the soldiers demobilized, the feeling of communion dissolved and there only remained feelings of defeat and disillusion or a little spurious joy; and Owen besides was dead.

And there comes another wave of French (decadent) influence, of bookishness, obscurity, intellectual superiority, and it looks at first sight as if we are in for a poetry more esoteric than that of the nineties. The leader is T. S. Eliot, an American, who had been influenced by the Imagists and especially by Ezra Pound; this influence was primarily technical, since the Imagists, as has been stated, ignored subject-matter. But Eliot's own poetry was not a mere experimenting in shape. When we examine his subject-matter we note the appearance here of the modern industrial city, of the Christian religion, of the background of European history—three things of which the Georgians appeared to be ignorant.

The Georgians at their best had shown fine observation of a limited range of objects and expressed honestly and pleasantly their reactions to such. Thus Edmund Blunden:

> apple-boughs as knarred as old toads' backs
> Wear their small roses ere a rose is seen. . . .

But the Georgians did not, as major poets do, use such experiences with a wider reference—as D. H. Lawrence does in his poems on animals or flowers or G. M. Hopkins in his poem on the kestrel. The Georgians had no world-view. Herein their nature-poetry differed from that of Wordsworth. One would not, of course, expect many people, especially nowadays, to be born Wordsworthians. European poetry now seems to be steadily returning towards the Greek tradition—

> The proper study of Mankind is Man

and not rustic man at that.

With Eliot we meet a poet who has a world-view and is interested in the study of mankind. His world-view is defeatist and he sees mankind through the glasses of a pedant, but he is at least civilized, synoptic, and—with allowance made for his pedantry—a realist. And for all his talk in his critical writings of impersonality, Eliot is a very personal poet. His early poems were studies from a corner; Eliot did not come out from his corner nor take sides, but he at least sat in his corner looking outwards, portraying the people nearest to him but seeing the contemporary world (and its implications of history) behind those people as their background. And this was a great advance on the corner-poets proper.

Mr. E. M. Forster tells of how he first read Eliot's poems ('Prufrock' and 'A Portrait of a Lady') during the War and found them

innocent of public-spiritness: they sang of private disgust and diffidence, and of people who seemed genuine because they were unattractive or weak. . . . Here was a protest, and a feeble one, and the more congenial for being feeble. For what, in that world of gigantic horror, was tolerable except the slighter gestures of dissent? . . . He who could turn aside to complain of ladies and drawing-rooms preserved a tiny drop of our self-respect, he carried on the human heritage.

Some ten years later less feeble protests were to be made by poets and the human heritage carried on rather differently. Eliot became notorious for his technique, but his technique was suited to his subject-matter:

> These fragments I have shor'd against my ruins

was always his early cry (till he took up Anglo-Catholicism) and his verse was carefully fragmentary to match the world as he perceived it. But the contemplation of a world of fragments becomes boring and Eliot's successors are more interested in tidying it up.

For Eliot's subject—the subject of all the poems down to and including 'The Hollow Men'—we may compare what Matthew Arnold said of his own subject-matter in *Empedocles on Etna* when rejecting it as not being properly *tragic*, from an edition of his poems:

What then are the situations, from the representation of which, though accurate, no poetical enjoyment can be derived? They are those in which the suffering finds no vent in action; in which a continuous state of mental distress is prolonged, unrelieved by incident, hope or resistance; in which there is everything to be endured, nothing to be done. In such situations there is inevitably something morbid, in the description of them something monotonous. When they occur in actual life, they are painful, not tragic; the representation of them in poetry is painful also.

This was an over-statement. Arnold, we must remember, would not have allowed himself to derive a 'poetical enjoyment' from satire. And there is plenty of the satirist in the earlier Eliot. Further, though the suffering finds no vent in action, Eliot has his foils for what is painful or squalid. The poet, as he says, is concerned with the 'boredom and the glory' of the contemporary world. Though there is little glory in 'Prufrock', the glories of religion and history are implicit in 'The Waste Land'.

'Prufrock' (a highbrow's social satire) was published in 1917. The *Poems* of 1920 were mainly a pedant's cynicism. 'The Waste Land', Eliot's most moving and most personal poem, was published in 1922, 'The Hollow Men' (sheer defeatism) in 1925, 'Ash-Wednesday' (Eliot's first positively Christian poem) in 1930. In 1932 there was published, edited by Michael Roberts, an anthology of poems by young poets, then hardly known to the public, who included W. H. Auden, Stephen Spender, Cecil Day-Lewis, John Lehmann, Julian Bell, William Plomer. Nearly all these poets, though unlike each other, were far more like each other than they were like Eliot. This was very significant, for Eliot since the War had had a vast influence on young poets, who had adopted both his method and his matter. The difference may be made clear by comparing Eliot's own remarks on modern poetry with those of Michael Roberts in his preface to *New Signatures*.

Eliot in an essay on the Metaphysical Poets (1921) wrote:

We can only say that it appears likely that poets in our civilisation, as it exists at present, must be *difficult*. Our civilisation comprehends great variety and complexity, and this variety and complexity, playing upon a refined sensibility, must produce various and complex results. The poet must become more and more comprehensive, more allusive, more indirect, in order to force, to dislocate if necessary, language into his meaning.

Michael Roberts (1932) wrote:

The solution of some too insistent problems may make it possible to write 'popular' poetry again: . . . because the poet will find that he can best express his newly-found attitude in terms of a symbolism which happens to be of exceptionally wide validity. . . . The poems in this book represent a clear reaction against esoteric poetry in which it is necessary for the reader to catch each recondite allusion.

These new poets, in fact, were boiling down Eliot's 'variety and complexity' and finding that it left them with certain comparatively clear-cut issues. Instead, therefore, of attempting an impressionist survey of the contemporary world—a world which impinges on one but which one cannot deal with, they were deliberately simplifying it, distorting it perhaps (as the man of action also has to distort it) into a world where one gambles upon practical ideals, a world in which one can take sides.

Their attitude, as Michael Roberts said in his preface, is more like that of the Greeks. It is controlled by the conception of man as a 'political animal'. 'Political animal' would, indeed, be a key-phrase to this poetry, for with the recognition that man is conditioned by economic factors and therefore needs the company of men *qua* community goes the recognition that man is a creature of strong physical instincts and affections, and therefore needs the company of men *qua* individuals. These poems do not, like so many politicians, think of human beings as cogs in a political machine but as organisms necessarily

dependent upon other organisms. Thomas Mann
said that 'Karl Marx must read Friedrich Hölderlin'. The poetry of Auden and Spender shows a
similar synthesis; they inherit from Marx on the
one hand and from D. H. Lawrence on the other.
Thus Spender in his critical book, *The Destructive
Element*, expressly advocates the synthesis of Marx-
ism and Freudian psychology. None of these poets
are unrealistically anarchist. They do not hanker
for an unconditioned existence. Freedom for them is
not freedom from conditions but the freedom to see
one's own conditions clearly and to work upon that
basis towards an end which is seen as necessary.

They cannot be called optimists, for they see that
there are always brute facts in opposition to their
progress. But they should not be called pessimists,
for they see that, while on all sides there is a vast
waste of effort among human beings, to be able to
waste effort like this implies an astonishing fund of
energy, and to be able to choose wrong so often
implies a capacity for choosing right. So when, as
often, their poems are gloomy, the gloom is tragic
rather than defeatist.

Tragedy implies a hero, and in the works of these
poets heroic values are once more being admitted.
Thus Auden:

> And further here and there, though many dead
> Lie under the poor soil, some acts are chosen
> Taken from recent winters; two there were
> Cleaned out a damaged shaft by hand, clutching
> The winch the gale would tear them from. . . .

Similarly, history is recognized as something

having a shape and still alive, something more than a mere accumulation of random and dead facts. Witness Spender's poem 'The Exiles', whose 'deeds and deaths are birds':

> The shattered dead whose veins are mineral
> We mine for here. . . .

or Auden:

> Consider the years of the measured world begun,
> The barren spiritual marriage of stone and water.
> Yet, O, at this very moment of our hopeless sigh
>
> .   .   .   .   .
>
> Some possible dream, long coiled in the ammonite's slumber
> Is uncurling, prepared to lay on our talk and kindness
> Its military silence, its surgeon's idea of pain;
>
> And out of the Future into actual history,
> As when Merlin, tamer of horses, and his lords to whom
> Stonehenge was still a thought, the Pillars passed
>
> And into the undared ocean swung north their prow,
> Drives through the night and star-concealing dawn
> For the virgin roadsteads of our hearts an unwavering keel.

The primary characteristic of these poets is that they are interested in a subject outside themselves— or at any rate in a subject which is not merely a subject for their poetry. This being so, it surprises many people that their manner should often appear esoteric—difficult syntax, difficult imagery, obscure allusions. The reasons for this are two—firstly, that, while reacting in the spirit from their predecessors— Eliot, Pound, the French Symbolists, Rilke—they have been much influenced by them in the letter (this is the manner in which they learned to write);

secondly, that, being poets, and not propagandists or journalists, they approach their subject, though an outside subject, through themselves. They will get their poetry more in order when they have got themselves in order, which in its turn may depend on a re-ordering of their society; they must not, however, wait for this last, for their relation with it is circular and they themselves, by writing, may in a tiny measure contribute to it.

La chair est triste, hélas! et j'ai lu tous les livres

wrote Mallarmé, as if the two things were essentially connected. Mallarmé was essentially a bookish poet, a rejecter. It is more elegant to be an out-and-out rejecter than an out-and-out accepter—such as Walt Whitman:

You shall no longer take things at second or third hand, nor look through the eyes of the dead, nor feed on the spectres in books,
You shall not look through my eyes either, nor take things from me,
You shall listen to all sides and filter them from yourself.

It would be fatal for poetry if all poets were to write on the Whitman recipe. It is the poet's job to filter things for his public. But the spirit of Whitman is more vital than the spirit of Mallarmé. There is a chance for poets to-day to retain the *élan vital* of Whitman or of Lawrence (though in Lawrence it is corrupt) but to girder it with a structure supplied partly by reason, partly by emotion intelligently canalized to an end, partly by the mere love of form.

M. Charles Mauron in his introduction to Roger Fry's translations from Mallarmé writes: 'Like all real poems, the poems of Mallarmé are compromises.' I should agree with the general statement but contend that Mallarmé did not compromise enough. That he should suggest rather than state is defensible as an attempt to represent the subtler shadings of life which are lost in direct statement. But Mallarmé goes farther than this—towards a 'pure poetry'. As M. Mauron points out, the experiences of life are for Mallarmé merely a jumping-off board into another kind of reality which, by the criteria of life, is unreal like the reality of the higher mathematics.

'Asking,' says M. Mauron, 'whatever spectacle was offered him by the street, the theatre, or his own home: "What does this mean?" *that is* [italics mine]: what arabesque can I trace, through dream, between the two or three facts which reality here presents to me, and which are to be justified by that arabesque? For, his obsession being concentrated on the movement of the mind and not on the actual data, it was in truth the former which justified the latter: instead of a curve being the means of relating facts one to another, the facts were meaningless except as points in an ideal line.'

This is a different escapism from that mentioned above. The writer who is predominantly realist or critical uses words to communicate the world that he knows or his thoughts about it. The escape-writer of the type who creates fantasies uses words to communicate the fairy-land world of his wishes. But Mallarmé is trying to drop communication; his poetry professes not to represent any world outside itself—real or fantastic—but itself to be a little world

of its own. The *method* in which he uses language
ceases to be a means towards an end and affects to be
an end in itself.

I would admit that poetry is something more than
mere communication and that *if* that 'something
more' could be abstracted from the whole it might
well prove to be that which makes the whole a poem.
But poetry is not like geometry. A poem is not an
abstracted circle but rather a solid ball. What makes
the ball a ball is its roundness—in Aristotle's phrase,
its formal cause—but it cannot dispense with its
material cause. A poem can only be made with
words and words are like wood or clay or rubber:
you can make a ball out of them but you cannot make
roundness out of them *and nothing but* roundness.

It seems to me, therefore, that Mallarmé's escapism, when analysed, approximates to the more common kind of escapism. He cannot abnegate the
poet's function of communication but by using words
peculiarly, in the profession that he is freeing them
from their meaning, he is merely freeing them so as
to evoke less rigid or less realistic meanings—building up not a higher mathematics or music but a
dream-world with a subtle mathematical or musical
structure.

The same kind of analysis could be applied to
Paul Valéry or to any other poets who claim to produce 'pure poetry'. I suspect that Miss Laura
Riding is one of these, for she calls herself 'a poet
who writes strictly for the reasons of poetry', and
says that 'existence in poetry becomes more real than
existence in time'. If this statement meant that it is

possible for a poem to give you a truer view of an
object or an experience than you might get in real
life when hustled against the object or experience
itself I might agree, but I suspect that Miss Riding
means something like what M. Mauron attributed to
Mallarmé. And I answer that this may be true of
higher mathematics or yoga or even music but that
I am sure it is not true of poetry (or, I should think,
of painting).

The poets of *New Signatures* have swung back, as
I have said, to the Greek preference for information
or statement. The first requirement is to have something to say, and after that you must say it as well as
you can. Now I should contend that, whatever their
professions, poets like Mallarmé and Rimbaud had
things which they wanted to say and which they said
as well as they could. And I should agree with those
who say paradoxically that the poet is often not completely sure what he is trying to say until he has said
it. He works up to his meaning by a dialectic of
purification. There is the thing A and his own reaction to it B, but as he is a poet (and, as a poet, only
properly or fully existent when making a poem) his
poet's reaction to A is not realized till the thing A has
been transported (a mysterious process) right into
his poem, when it is no longer A but a, and with this
a is fused his own poetic reaction to it—β. Or, more
strictly, instead of the still segregated A and B there
is now only the resulting poetic unity $a\beta$.

But, all this being admitted, I still maintain that
some poets have from the start a much clearer idea
than others of what they want to say, and that this is

because the thing which they are writing about is something more 'objective' or palpable, more public, more clearly recognizable within some traditional scheme of values. Their readers can tumble to $\alpha\beta$ because they recognize the A behind it and have themselves had the experience B. Whereas poets like Rimbaud and Mallarmé are attempting to present a thing A which hardly exists at all until it is embodied (I say 'embodied' deliberately instead of 'informed') by the *poet's* final reaction to it—β. But in poets like Auden and Spender the solid basis of A and B persists and is recognizable.

Yeats is a poet who has a foot in both worlds for (1) he is, like Walter Pater, his master, a great enthusiast for 'style' and for the dream-world of art; he remembers forgotten beauty. In his earlier days he expressly advocated 'escape'. In an essay on *The Symbolism of Poetry* (1900) he wrote:

With this return to imagination, this understanding that the laws of art, which are the hidden laws of the world [note the inversion], can alone bind the imagination, would come a change of style, and we would cast out of serious poetry those energetic rhythms, as of a man running [e.g. Locksley Hall?], which are the invention of the will with its eyes always on something to be done or undone [contrast Aristotle's demand for *action* in drama]; and we would seek out those wavering, meditative, organic rhythms, which are the embodiment of the imagination that neither desires nor hates, because it has done with time. [Remember that Yeats considers Ibsen the arch-enemy of poetry—a judgement with which most of the younger poets would strongly disagree.]

This wish to be 'done with time' reminds us of the

aspirations of such poets as Mallarmé and Valéry, but the later Yeats has recognized the necessity of the descent into time, of 'desecration and the lover's night'. And as for desiring and hating, he even writes: 'I study hatred with great diligence' [notice that, correspondingly, his rhythms waver less], and most of his later poetry embodies strong preferences for one kind of life or person over another.

For (2) even in an early essay Yeats writes of a great discovery:

> We should write out our own thoughts in as nearly as possible the language we thought them in, as though in a letter to an intimate friend. We should not disguise them in any way; for our lives give them force as the lives of people in plays give force to their words. . . . 'If I can be sincere and make my language natural, and without becoming discursive like a novelist and so indiscreet and prosaic,' I said to myself, 'I shall, if good luck or bad luck make my life interesting, be a great poet; for it will be no longer [N.B.] a matter of literature at all.' Yet when I re-read those early poems which gave me so much trouble, I find little but romantic convention, unconscious drama. *It is so many years before one can believe enough in what one feels even to know what the feeling is* [italics mine].

Yeats is not, like Burns, a poet of strong physical emotions, and it has, I think, taken him a long time to find out what his feelings are; perhaps even now he sometimes deceives himself. But in writing about historical events with which he has been connected (see that fine poem 'Easter 1916') or people of interest whom he has known intimately (Lady Gregory, Major Robert Gregory, Synge, his own relations), he produces something which is not merely a matter of literature.

But Yeats's world-view is so esoteric that he can only escape from literature at odd moments. He believes in discipline but in a discipline which, as is made clear in *Dramatis Personae*, is entirely egotistical:

There is a relation between discipline and the theatrical sense. If we cannot imagine ourselves as different from what we are [no question here of *making* ourselves different] and assume that second self, we cannot impose a discipline upon ourselves, though we may accept one from others. Active virtue as distinguished from the passive acceptance of a current code [why *passive*?] is therefore theoretical, consciously dramatic, the wearing of a mask.

Opposed to this theatrical discipline, this cult of the Mask, which goes with Yeats's admiration for aristocracies is the more democratic discipline, accepted *from without*, of *New Signatures*. This discipline can be roughly said to be *a posteriori* where that from within is *a priori*. It involves, firstly, an honest survey of the contemporary world, an unflinching recognition of its evils and deficiencies, but, secondly, a recognition of that world's potentialities for good; the poet, if only by pointing out where the actual world does and does not realize the ideal, will be at the same time realist and idealist, honest while taking sides, indirectly a militant.

Those philosophers who, like Schopenhauer, have drawn too sweeping a distinction between the actual and the ideal have thought of the ideal world either as a substitute for the actual or, at best, as something to be abstracted from the actual world by, it may be, the artist, the aesthete, the philosopher, or the mystic. Art in particular has often been regarded recently as an escape from the actual to some transcendent reality on the pattern of Plato's Forms, whereas Marxist materialism ignores *transcendent* realities and is therefore a good creed for the artist who must move in a concrete world.

The poets of *New Signatures*, unlike Yeats and Eliot, are emotionally partisan. Yeats proposed to turn his back on desire and hatred; Eliot sat back and watched other peoples' emotions with ennui and an ironical self-pity:

I keep my countenance,
I remain self-possessed
Except when a street piano mechanical and tired
Reiterates some worn-out common song
With the smell of hyacinths across the garden
Recalling things that other people have desired [italics mine].

The whole poetry, on the other hand, of Auden, Spender, and Day-Lewis implies that they have desires and hatreds of their own and, further, that they think some things *ought* to be desired and others hated.

This does not mean, however, that their world is a crude world of black and white, of sheep and goats. Auden, for example, has the advantage of seeing the world both in terms of psycho-analysis and of a Marxian doctrine of progress [see above]. Thereby nearly all the detail in the world becomes significant for him. For Auden *qua* psychologist anything, almost. will become (*a*) an example or symbol of a neurosis demanding cure, or (*b*) an example or symbol of how a neurosis produces good (for Auden believes that all progress is due to neurotic restlessness). For Auden *qua* Marxist, on the other hand, nearly anything will be either (*a*) a product of the enemy, of reaction, bad and to be fought against, or (*b*) a relic of an obsolete past, once perhaps good but now bad and to be deplored, though often with reverence or affection, or (*c*) an earnest of better things, a pioneer of the future—or else a symbol of one of these three types. It will be seen that the neurotic who needs curing will often be identifiable with the political enemy, while the productive neurotics will include the political reformers. Auden, therefore, cannot, like many politicians, be accused of having crude animosities. The issues are simplified but the people remain complex. And Auden shows great sympathy with people.

Modern poetry is often accused of being ugly and sordid, morbid and cynical. Witness the early poems of Eliot:

> The morning comes to consciousness
> Of faint stale smells of beer
> From the sawdust-trampled street
> With all its muddy feet that press
> To early coffee-stands.
> With the other masquerades
> That time resumes,
> One thinks of all the hands
> That are raising dingy shades
> In a thousand furnished rooms.

Those who attack such writing would agree with

Matthew Arnold that sordor, apathy, unheroic defeat are unfit subjects for poetry. Those who defend it frequently defend it as satire (having admitted, to start with, that satire can be poetry). I would say that pure satire is a low form of writing because it does not admit any sympathy with its subject, but would add that little modern poetry is pure satire.

Mr. Wyndham Lewis in his book *Men without Art* maintains that satire is the proper genre for this age. He makes, however, the important qualification that satire, as he conceives it, can be non-ethical, non-partisan. It is satire for its own sake *and allied to tragedy* (I would certainly agree that Eliot's satire is allied to tragedy). The satirist need grind no axe, according to Mr. Lewis, and his concern will be rather with the outsides of people than their insides. Analysis of Mr. Lewis's book shows that his pure satire approximates to other forms of pure art or pure poetry, or any writing which is practised entirely 'for its own sake'.

Wyndham Lewis is basically a pessimist, thinking of human beings as doomed animals or determinist machines. His theory of satire is based on this view and he finds plenty of evidence to support it in contemporary practice. Thus Eliot is always stressing the automatic, nightmare, machine qualities of people (compare Joyce in *Ulysses*):

So the hand of the child, automatic,
Slipped out and pocketed a toy that was running along the key.
I could see nothing behind that child's eye.

On which the irreverent might comment, 'I bet he couldn't.'

Eliot's early poems juxtapose values and realities, but the two are always in divorce. The works of art and literature and religion do not fall on the side of reality; an Atlantic separates their Old World from the crude, sordid, evil New World of Sweeney.

> A lustreless protrusive eye
>   Stares from the protozoic slime
> At a perspective of Canaletto. . . .

Rather romantic and bookish conceptions of Past Glory, Ideal Beauty, and Goodness, the pure worlds of Art and Religion are played off against a romantic debasement of the impure world around us.

The formula for such poems—a fancy world set off against an ironic statement—had already been found by A. E. Housman:

> The fairies break their dances
>   And leave the printed lawn,
> And up from India glances
>   The silver sail of dawn.

> The candles burn their sockets,
>   The blinds let through the day,
> The young man feels his pockets
>   And wonders what's to pay.

Wyndham Lewis maintains that it is the artist's or writer's business to depict the Without of people and not their Within. This principle leads to the presentation of much that is sordid or trivial. The presentation of the Without without reference to the values of the Within will (as Mass Observation tends to) give results which are only quantitatively true. Thus the half-hour a man spends in the lavatory

will be given more prominence than the ten minutes
he spends arranging flowers.

Nearly all poets, however, have selected surface
details with reference to inner, or spiritual, criteria.
The heroic moods were given more prominence than
the everyday moods of boredom or irritation because
in the latter man did not seem to be exercising such a
specifically human faculty, and most poets, following
the Greeks, have been more interested in man functioning as man than in man as an animal or a machine
or a visual mass based on the cube and the cylinder.
Baudelaire wrote about ennui but his ennuis were
heroic. The truthful representation of ennui can be
valuable as a foil, not a foil to a fancy world, but
a patch of drab in the real world which also has its
lights and colours.

The poets of *New Signatures* are interested in Man
Functioning. They select their detail (for they still,
like the Imagists but not for the same reason, believe
in particulars) in order to illustrate the workings of
vital principles. Original Sin is for them more
cardinal than Original Inertia.

The poet is once again to make his response as a
whole. On the one side is concrete living—not just
a conglomeration of animals or machines, mere flux, a
dissolving hail of data, but a system of individuals
determined by their circumstances, a concrete, therefore, of sensuous fact and what we may call 'uni-
versals'; on the other side is a concrete poet—not
just an eye or a heart or a brain or a solar plexus, but
the whole man reacting with both intelligence and
emotion (which is how we react to anything in

ordinary life) to experiences, and on this basis presenting something which is (*a*) communication, a record, but is also (*b*) a creation—having a new unity of its own, something in its shape which makes it poetry.

MY CASE-BOOK: CHILDHOOD

i. *Introductory*

THE poet is a specialist in something which every one practises. Herein poetry differs from the other arts. Every one does not practise music or painting or even dancing, but every one without exception puts together words poetically every day of his life. There are only two ways of using language —the scientific and the poetic. Science attempts to record or analyse phenomena objectively without personal bias or emotion and without *formal* considerations other than those of sheer utility; purely scientific language is a means to knowledge and in no sense an end. Very few people use language frequently in this way. Most people make most of their remarks at least partly for the love of talking. Very few remarks are intended wholly or merely to convey information about outside objects or events. We are speaking poetically rather than scientifically when we 'make conversation', when we make a joke, when we use cliché metaphors or racy slang, when we express any emotion either by meiosis or hyperbole, when we let off steam by using bad language or surplus superlatives, when we say, 'It *would* rain just now just when I've hung my washing out.'

This being so, it is regrettable that so many people should think of poetry as an abnormal activity and of the poet as a freak growth moving in the sphere of fancy rather than fact, and subject to a miracle called inspiration. Every one is not able, or inclined, to *write* poetry in the narrower sense any more than every one is qualified to take part in a walking race. But just as all of us can and do walk, so all of us can and do use language poetically.

The majority of people do not want to read poetry any more than they want to watch walking races. They get enough poetry and walking in the course of their daily lives. But there are people who feel that this everyday activity is of such interest and importance that they wish to practise it as specialists or have it practised by specialists in a field where they can get a good look at it.

The poet has no greater number of muscles than the ordinary conversationalist; he merely has more highly developed muscles and better co-ordination. And he practises his activity according to a stricter set of rules. But he has one great point in common with the ordinary conversationalist; they both use language primarily in order to convey a meaning (though not, as I have said, a purely scientific meaning). In the same way the muscles both of athletes and ordinary men are equally intended for the purpose of moving their limbs. Now the poet, to start with, is at a disadvantage compared with the conversationalist because the latter can put over his meaning with the help of tone of voice or facial expression, and to hearers who are 'in the know' with him in so far as they share his company at one particular spot in place and time. The poet has to turn his disadvantage into an advantage; his limitations supply him with rules and his rules supply him with shape. The absence of the spoken voice, of the face, of the particular place and time, must be compensated by a far greater precision of diction, by greater architectonic.

But the rules or 'laws' of poetry are only tentative devices, an approximate scheme. There is no Sinaitic recipe for poetry, for the individual poem is the norm. If we judge poems according to hard-and-fast rules we shall find greater distinctions between one kind of poem and another than are there in fact. My object in writing this essay is partly to show that one and the same poetic activity produces different forms in adaptation to circumstances. There is no such break between 'modern' poetry and traditional poetry as a superficial view might suggest.

In so far as possible I wish not to bring in metaphysics. Thus the differentia of poetry is often said to be the collocation of dissimilars in a new or previously unperceived identity. Any one who thinks about it will see that any two data chosen at random from the world have something at least in common, and are to some extent—if only numerically—distinct. To make the above definition at all useful we have to descend from metaphysics into history and inquire what at a particular time are the stereotyped similarities and what are the new similarities which demand to be pointed out. And the artist should only point out those which are within a reasonable range of vision. (I leave the question as to whether the range of vision which is reasonable is that of the

artist himself or of the top level, however defined, of
contemporary culture or of the ideal normal man or
of the actual community or of any particular section
of it. I feel myself that the poet should imagine as
his audience an ideal normal man who is an educated
member of his own community and is basically at
one with the poet in his attitude to life.)

Literary criticism is usually, and rightly, founded
on literary history (though critics are mistaken in
that they often too rigorously separate literary history
from social or economic history). The literary history
—the 'influences'—behind modern poetry has often
been treated by critics, so I intend instead to submit
some literary autobiography, i.e. the history of my
own reactions to and demands from poetry, in reading and writing it, over a number of years starting
from early childhood. I think that this may throw
a sidelight on the evolution of modern poetry in the
same way that embryonic physiology throws a sidelight on the evolution of species or child-psychology
throws a sidelight on adult activities.

I disagree with those who, like Mr. Eliot, contend
that for a young boy, an adolescent, and an adult
poetry respectively is three things different in kind.
Eliot in *The Use of Poetry and the Use of Criticism*
writes:

> 'I put forward the conjecture that the majority of children,
> up to say twelve or fourteen, are capable of a certain enjoy-
> ment of poetry; that at or about puberty the majority of these
> find little further use for it, but that a small minority of them
> then find themselves possessed of a craving for poetry which
> is wholly different from any enjoyment experienced before.'

I would contend in opposition that the adolescent's reaction to poetry has an identity with the child's reaction, just as, according to modern psychologists, sex-life does not begin at adolescence but at birth.

I find in looking back that from childhood my own reactions to poetry have changed, been widened, intensified, generally developed, but that this development has been continuous, and poetry for me, correspondingly, has suffered no mutation in kind.

All experiment is made on a basis of tradition; all tradition is the crystallization of experiment. Having during my childhood and adolescence visited both the poles of traditionalism and of free-lance experimentation, I feel that a survey of these journeys and a return from these towards a conception of living tradition (distinguished from dead traditionalism) may illustrate *in parvo* and more simply the interflux of extremist principles in modern poetry which is gradually resolving itself towards that same conception.

ii

When I was a small child I preferred dolls and bears to machines. I correlate with this the fact that I preferred language 'with style on it' to language which merely gave information. My father was a clergyman, and from a very early age I was fascinated by the cadences and imagery of the Bible.

Much that I remember about myself must be true of most children. Our intellectual tastes become progressively differentiated as we grow older; more and more of the side-shows fail to hold our attention, which becomes concentrated on one or two chief interests (thus Darwin complained that his taste for music had become atrophied). Thus nearly all children have a feeling for rhythm in words, for the delicate pattern of nursery rhymes. Many adults have lost this feeling and, if they read verse at all, demand a far cruder music than that which they once appreciated.

We also tend to lose our vivid reactions to pictorial imagery. A phrase no longer automatically summons up a picture. This is partly because the phrase grows stale. When the words 'grass' and 'green' are comparatively new to us the phrase 'green grass' at once overwhelms us with greenness. And we have not yet complacently accepted that everything is as it is for we are at the stage when we ask, '*Why* is the grass green?' The adult when he sees a truism passes by on the other side. You have to shake an adult to get a reaction out of him. Hence the constant endeavour of sophisticated poetry to *surprise* its readers.

To use the distinction, which I have already carefully qualified, between 'escape' and 'criticism of life', children's poetry is on the whole escapist, though nursery rhymes (some of which even originated as political lampoons) do contain for the child a 'criticism' of his world. That the two elements are interlocked is shown by the death or physical torture motif, so common in both fairy-stories and nursery rhymes. It is legitimate to say that such motifs being treated in a two-dimensional tapestry manner (as they also are in detective stories or Hollywood melodramas) need not be taken seriously because it is

all fun, make-believe—we are escaping into a world
of thrills but minus the pain with which, in real life,
such thrills are usually accompanied. But it is also
legitimate to say that the child, being full of self-
assertion, indignation, animosity, and at times a
sadist, likes to work off on these fictitious victims
the spite which, consciously or unconsciously, he
feels towards his nurse or parents. Nursery rhymes
are full of people who fall down wells or jump into
bramble-bushes and scratch out both their eyes. The
humour of childhood is the Hobbesian feeling of
self-glory experienced at others' discomfiture. Much
adult humour is of the same kind. Poldy Bloom
hooted from the pub in *Ulysses* is a successor of
'Humpty-Dumpty'.

Similarly with sex. Modern psychology has, as I
said above, exploded the idea that sex-life begins at
adolescence. The love-poetry, such as it is, of nursery rhymes is mainly escapist because it is all sugar
and no salt, but the child who reads it has a foretaste
of the feelings he will have when reading love-poetry
proper. The attention in nursery rhymes is usually
focused on accessories—rings on her fingers and
bells on her toes—and modern children are on the
way to being dress-fetishists. When I was about 7
I was chiefly attracted to ladies by their accessories,
and I used to have dreams about a lady whom I saw
in church wearing long white gloves up to her elbows.
'Mary, Mary,' with her garden was desirable to me,
and the Queen in the Parlour eating bread and honey
(which had a seductive flavour of naughtiness). And
so was the King of Spain's daughter.

At the same age I met with hymns—my first melancholy poetry. The most melancholy hymn to me (though this was partly due to associations) was 'There is a green hill far away'. I pictured a small round hill, a desolately intense green (as green grass in Ireland can be desolate), very much like a mound in a field near my home called 'The Fairy Mount'. I thought that 'Without a city wall' meant that there was no wall round it, and this added to its treeless bleakness. 'He only can unlock the door' called up an actual door—I think with studs on it—like a church door.

At the age of about 7 I had an anthology of verse which included some of Blake's 'Songs of Innocence', some songs from Shakespeare, 'The Poplars are Felled', and ballads like 'Sir Patrick Spens'. Nostalgic poetry like 'The Poplars are Felled' always appealed to me very strongly because, as far back as I can remember, I was always looking back to some preceding, hardly remembered period as a kind of Golden Age. At a very early age I always had a feeling of nostalgia if I saw boats in the distance on the sea and also (but not so strong) when I looked at a picture of Highland cattle in a mist on a mountain. Some of Moore's songs (e.g. 'The Meeting of the Waters') evoked in me similar feelings.

'Sir Patrick Spens' gave me a pleasant terror, as did 'The Wife of Usher's Well'. The dialect words which I hardly understood enhanced this. On the whole I reacted to these ballads much as I do now. The poem of Blake which struck me most was 'The Chimney-Sweeper'. I liked its metre and saw its story in a succession of very vivid pictures. Shakespeare's songs I did not like very much, though 'When icicles hang by the wall . . .' gave me an intense physical feeling of winter. 'Toll for the Brave' impressed me, largely because I liked the name Kempenfelt. 'Death the Leveller' horrified me.

The first book I read which contained poems all by the same poet was a small selection of Tennyson's lyrics, a tiny book bound in velvet (even then the velvet seemed to me in keeping). I remember especially 'It is the miller's daughter', which left me cold, and 'The Lady of Shalott', which I liked very much. As with 'Sir Patrick Spens', the music, the pictures, and the atmosphere of 'The Lady of Shalott' affected me then almost exactly as they do now.

> Willows whiten, aspens quiver,
> Little breezes dusk and shiver

then, as now, recalled most pleasantly to me a familiar experience. But I am no longer frightened or awed by the poem as a whole, for I realize that this piece, though dressy, is fancy-dress at its best.

From the age of 7 I wrote poems myself. What I was chiefly interested in was the pattern of the words. My recipe for a poem was simple—use 'thou' instead of 'you' and make the ends of the lines rhyme with each other; no specific emotion or 'poetic' content required. Here is a poem about a live parrot which I had seen in a neighbour's house:

> O parrot, thou hast grey feathers
> Which thou peckest in all weathers.
> And thy curled beak
> Could make me squeak;

Thy tail I admire
As red as the fire
And as red as a carrot,
Thy tail I admire,
Thou cross old parrot.

This seems to me now to be better writing than
much which I afterwards wrote in the fervour of my
adolescence. There is a nucleus of observed fact,
and my naïve idea that putting anything into rhyme
makes it a poem at least enabled me to convey this
fact in memorable form (I use the word memorable
in its literal sense, which is its basic sense, because
I find this poem easy to remember).

In writing poems like this I never felt any emotion
such as I felt when reading most of those above mentioned or when looking at the boats in the distance.
I was interested in the pattern of the words and, secon-
darily, in some piece of information which I thought
would go nicely into pattern. This matter-of-fact
attitude was later destroyed jointly by sentimentalism
and snobbism, but now that the 'Sturm und Drang'
of my adolescence is over I tend to think again that
the normal business of poetry is the conveying of
information through certain kinds of word-patterns
and that it is a mistake to assess poetry primarily in
terms of emotion. If we investigate it, of course, no
information in ordinary life (as distinct from science)
is conveyed *entirely* without emotion; there must, to
start with, be some emotional reason why we choose
to convey *x* rather than *y*. It is impossible for a
human being to feel a single emotion without *some*
exercise of thought at the same time, and it is im-

possible to think a single thought without also expe-
riencing some degree of emotion, however tiny (I
have exempted science from emotion but not the
individual scientist). What I would object to in
Wordsworth's conception of poetry is the implication that only intense emotions or emotions implying
a certain moral dignity are fit to be embodied in
poems. Much of the greatest poetry implies such
emotions, but it is vicious to turn the characteristic
of a certain kind of poetry, even the greatest, into a
sine qua non for all poetry.

iii

When I went to an English preparatory school at
the age of 10 (in 1917) I was given Palgrave's
Golden Treasury, and this was my chief verse-reading
for two years. During this period I underwent a
coarsening of taste and a growing preference for
what Yeats calls those 'crude, violent rhythms as of
a man running'. Like most boys of that age, I liked
the flashier heroics—'The Burial of Sir John Moore',
'Hohenlinden', 'The Battle of Naseby', 'The Execu-
tion of Montrose'.

The verse which forms the bulk of *The Golden
Treasury* is much less *natural* verse than that of
nursery rhymes. The running trochees and dactyls
of ordinary English speech give place to those
heavier latinized iambics which dominate our literary verse. And *The Golden Treasury*, though an excellent collection, has much too narrow a range as an
anthology for boys. There is too big a gap between
these formal self-conscious poems and the nursery

rhymes of their earlier years. Blake's songs might have helped to bridge the gap, and I should also throw into it a quantity of light verse and of modern folk-poetry such as the ballads of American cowboys. (Such an anthology for boys has recently been compiled by John Garrett and W. H. Auden, entitled *The Poet's Tongue*. This goes to the other extreme and has too high a percentage of light verse, comic verse, nonsense, and doggerel. But it should at least give boys a more catholic conception of poetry and save them from 'Noli Me Tangere'.)

The great majority of poems in *The Golden Treasury* related to events or emotions of which I had no experience—for example, all the martial poems, which were therefore—for me at any rate—poetry of escape. On the other hand, Herrick's 'Whenas in silks my Julia goes' geared in with my ordinary life, for I had seen with admiration people going in silks or something like them. Out of the whole book I preferred, at about the age of 11, the earlier and later poems to those in the middle. I disliked most of the pieces from the seventeenth and the eighteenth centuries, and the Romantic Revival bored me with the exception of some poems by Scott and —more surprisingly—by Wordsworth. I liked 'The Grammarian's Funeral', Fitzgerald's 'Omar Khayyam', Swinburne's 'Forsaken Garden', 'To Althea from Prison', 'Go Fetch to me a Pint o' Wine', 'Fear no more the heat o' the sun', and 'The Dowie Houms o' Yarrow'. And I liked, because it reminded me of church, Drummond's poem on St. John the Baptist.

I liked the above poems for various reasons. Browning gave me fascinating rhymes, 'Omar Khayyam' gave me neat and easy images and an epicureanism which I already found sympathetic, Swinburne gave me sensuous rhythm and nostalgia (I thought of overrun gardens which I had seen in Ireland). And I liked an obvious contrast:

> Golden lads and girls all must,
> As chimney-sweepers, come to dust.

The word 'golden' in itself was very evocative. Even now words like 'gold' and 'roses' tend to strike me as if written in block capitals, and in writing myself I have to avoid playing to this primitive reaction which obviously leads to abuses.

The first classical poems in the grand manner which impressed me were Dryden's 'Song for St. Cecilia's Day' and 'Alexander's Feast'—largely because they were magnificently read aloud by the headmaster. They had for me the pomp of certain hymns without their chilly sanctity. I liked especially the lines:

> Through all the compass of the notes it ran,
> The diapason closing full in man.

A controlled flamboyance of diction has always moved me, so that I have never subscribed to the Wordsworthian exclusive crusade for homespun.

The first long poem which I enjoyed and re-read for pleasure was 'The Lay of the Last Minstrel'. I did not like the other long poems of Scott. I am glad to say that in heroic verse I always preferred the Border ballads to Campbell or Macaulay. I enjoyed Macaulay very much, but he left a taste in the mouth as if I had eaten too many sweets. I think that I (unconsciously) missed in him the elasticity of the ballads and their savour of the earth. Kipling's 'Barrack-Room Ballads' won me completely, but they, too, have at least an element of earth in them.

I began to like point in verse—for example, Peacock's 'The mountain sheep are sweeter . . . '. I liked the *Ingoldsby Legends* and should no doubt have liked comic limericks but cannot remember having heard any. This love of point is, I fancy, common to boys of preparatory-school age who are for the most part fond of showing off and are more interested in knowing the names of butterflies than in observing the texture of their wings. It is the Latin period of our boyhood.

I never as a child read the nonsense limericks of Edward Lear, but I feel that at the age of 12 I should have preferred the ordinary limerick (*a*) because the content is not so 'childish', (*b*) because it is 'cleverer' —the end rhyme does not, as in Lear, repeat the first rhyme. I now think that though the new end rhyme is obviously a great asset to the kind of limerick which is essentially witty—an epigram or a lampoon—Lear's scheme is more suited to the limerick *as lyric*. It gives a better balanced and more assured statement; we do not anxiously wait for the virtuoso ending. Lear's limerick stands to the wit-limerick as the *Greek Anthology* stands to Martial. A preparatory schoolboy would certainly prefer Martial.

iv

I first achieved a highbrow attitude to poetry when I was 12. A young man from Oxford came to my school as a master and taught us English literature in the grand manner. He taught us that a critical appreciation of poetry was the main characteristic of a gentleman. He read aloud to us Keats, Shelley, Rupert Brooke, and even (with a slight sneer) 'The Rape of the Lock'. Keats became very popular with the boys, who responded quickly (as was demanded of them) to his sensuous and pictorial qualities— 'sweet peas on tiptoe for a flight' or 'blanched linen, smooth and lavender'd'. The same qualities we liked in Lycidas—'the Pansie freak't with jet', though I myself always, if I remember rightly, preferred Lycidas to Keats—partly because it was more sonorous, partly because it had a grim side to it; Keats had shadows but Milton had iron—the 'fatal and perfidious Bark', 'the grim Woolf with privy paw'.

The new master told us that it was vulgar to admire Kipling or Macaulay's lays. Poetry should contain true emotion, should be about beautiful things, and should offer an escape from the drabness of ordinary life. He chanted aloud Rupert Brooke's

> Then they'll know, poor fools, they'll know
> One moment what it is to love

and we responded with a delightful feeling of self-glory and contempt for the poor fools.

He also taught us some technical dogma, e.g. that in English verse double rhymes can only rarely be used, except for humorous purposes, and triple rhymes almost never. The only serious poem, he said, in which triple rhymes were used successfully was Hood's 'Bridge of Sighs'. One of the boys went round the school shouting the 'Bridge of Sighs' in the jolliest possible manner at the top of his voice, and since then, in spite of the master, it has seemed to me that the form of this poem is not properly wedded to its content.

The influence of this master was both good and bad. He gave us a great interest in the Romantic Revival but he narrowed still further than Palgrave our conception of poetry. He endorsed Matthew Arnold's stigma on the 'Age of Prose and Reason' (Pope was the 'arch-enemy') and made us unwilling to confess admiration for poems which were not obviously emotional, for poems written in dialect or containing prosy phrases, for poems which broke certain technical rules, for poems which mentioned anything 'ugly'. He held up for our contempt Kipling's lines about dancing with 'blowsy housemaids'; housemaids were to be taboo. Further, he encouraged us to think that Greek mythology or a mythology of some kind was almost necessary to poetry. Keats's nymphs could always walk in where the housemaids were banned.

On the strength of this teaching I read before leaving my preparatory school 'Endymion', 'Hyperion', and most of 'Paradise Lost', and 'The Faerie Queene', but I never read Chaucer or even heard him spoken of as important. As for Wordsworth, he was graded far below Keats. I required poetic diction and dream-figures. Blake's 'Chimney Sweeper' was now too vulgar, too grotesque. I wanted 'La Belle Dame Sans Merci'. And self-pity had become an important factor. Keats was very sorry for himself. It had always been easy and pleasant to be sorry for oneself; now we knew that it was also a poetic occupation.

III

MY CASE-BOOK: PUBLIC SCHOOL

i

I LEFT my preparatory school in 1921 owning
volumes of Shelley, Matthew Arnold, Scott, and
the *Oxford Book of English Verse*. On going to a
public school, Marlborough, I continued reading
the poetry of the Romantic Revival and Spenser,
whom I liked because he was musical and the story
went on and on. (Though sympathizing with the
present-day demand for concentration and economy
in poetry, I have never conceded to the extremists
that a great book is necessarily a great evil or that
mere decoration is necessarily vicious.) Spenser's
characters I certainly found thin after Malory, whom
I knew well, but I liked this escape world of knights
and dragons and refused to be put off by the allegory.
I did not wish to use my brains too much on poetry
and I let myself be lulled by Spenser's leisurely
enumerations:

> The Laurell, meed of mightie Conquerours
> And Poets sage, the Firre that weepeth still,
> The Willow worn of forlorne Paramours,
> The Eugh obedient to the bender's will,
> The Birch for shaftes, the Sallow for the mill,
> The Mirrhe swete bleeding in the bitter wound,
> The warlike Beech, the Ash for nothing ill,
> The fruitfull Olive, and the Platane round,
> The carver Holme, the Maple seeldom inward sound.

Such purely descriptive writing I was accustomed to in Virgil and, though it did not conform to the emotional doctrine of poetry which I had been taught, I liked it for the pattern and the pictures. In Virgil I often found that the most attractive parts were the similes, and a Virgilian simile tends to be expanded for its own sake, details being introduced which in no way illuminate the subject which occasioned the simile.

During my first year at Marlborough I began reading Homer, whom I at once recognized as richer than Virgil or Spenser, more congenial than Milton. I discovered that narrative poetry can retain its colour and dignity while dealing with people who, whatever their titles, their exceptional beauty and prowess, are much like ordinary people in their squabbles, greeds, and jealousies. I had read most of the tragedies of Shakespeare, but Shakespeare's characters seemed often to be either too much on the high horse or else flat on the ground. Homer gave me an example of verse-writing which was homogeneous but yet elastic enough to represent much of life's variety. I have noticed since that many modern theories of poetry could not make room for Homer. Many people generalize about poetry when they only mean lyric poetry. And Colonel Lawrence had at least the courage of his convictions when he denied that the 'Odyssey' was poetry.

At this same time I began reading some of the 'Odes of Horace', who also would be disallowed as a poet by many modern critics and is sometimes even disallowed by name. 'It does not ring true' people say of him as they say of Villon. What should be remembered is that the *attitude* in Horace, as in many Latin poets, is something consciously applied—one more convention within which the poet has to work. People misunderstand Horace because they miss the grain of salt and because they demand of him the directness and simplicity of a purely lyrical poet, whereas Horace is a contemplative poet writing odes which have something of the involved pattern of Pindar, though on a much smaller scale. As a boy I liked the glitter of Horace—O fons Bandusiae splendidior vitro—and admired his tidiness, realizing that English with its articles and lack of inflexions could hardly ever equal Horace either in concentration or in subtlety of word-order.

From the age of 14 to 16 I read poetry lazily. My emotions were less excited than when the master at my other school had read aloud to us Keats or Lycidas; the pictures called up were less clear than when I had been 7. I read for curiosity and for snob reasons. I was too self-conscious to write any poems myself except occasional comic verses which at least allowed me the pleasure of making patterns with words.

At the age of 16, when I was more ready to fall in love with people, I began to read poetry especially with a view to getting substitute sensations from it. I read the Georgian anthologies but found them unsatisfying except for a few lusher pieces like Ralph Hodgson's 'Bull' or Turner's poem about 'Chimborazo, Cotopaxi'. I liked Flecker's Oriental bazaar romanticism and the wistful 'magic' of De la Mare. I also liked a much larger quantity of bad poetry than previously, such as 'The Forest of Wild Thyme' by

Alfred Noyes, which rang all the bells of my nostalgia and self-pity. I read the 'Shropshire Lad', my lack of sexual experience answering gladly to its cynicism, and I read 'The Land of Heart's Desire' and 'The Countess Cathleen' by Yeats.

> The wind blows out of the gates of the day,
> The wind blows over the lonely of heart,
> And the lonely of heart is withered away.

These lines gave me uplift, for I fancied myself lonely of heart. I wrote a poem myself called 'Death of a Prominent Business Man', who was set to his discredit against a background of rain-swept rocks and heather.

Shortly afterwards I wrote a poem about the Twilight of the Gods in Valhalla, beginning:

> It was the last night of all their nights,
> They knew it well, so well. . . .

I was now thoroughly romanticist and could not have bothered myself even with Spenser; his properties were romantic but there was not enough outcry. I went back to Shelley, whom I had never yet preferred to Keats but who now suited my mood. For about a year and a half I thought of Shelley as *the* great poet. While I was 17 I wrote, as I think many people do when they are 17, a number of Shelleyan poems defying or renouncing everyday life and its codes.

On the other hand, snob values now became more powerful and I began debating questions of form. Up to my 17th birthday I was prepared to write poetry in any form and rather liked choosing an intricate traditional form such as the sonnet. But during the next year I became more and more beset with doubts as to whether these forms were adapted to what I had to say and whether it was really done to use such and such forms at all. So in the summer of 1925, when I wrote a long poem for a school competition I wrote it in free verse.

I had read hardly any free verse and mine was really dissipated blank verse, but I enjoyed writing it, for I had plenty to say and I liked to see the phrases pick themselves, unhampered by a rigid form, and I liked varying my cadences. I think that I was probably following a quite healthy instinct to compromise between traditional blank verse and the rhythms of ordinary speech. Thus the last line of this poem was:

The Venétian blinds and the hót dáy cóoling.

When I later read Gerard Manley Hopkins's account of his own metrical experiments I felt that in breaking down an old technical dogma he was tending to turn his new, and quite legitimate, conveniences into a new dogma of his own (see Chap. VII).

I had therefore, before I was 18, become interested in being fashionably modern. A school-friend of mine was very interested in painting, but especially in the post-impressionists. So, knowing nothing about painting, I began my acquaintance with it at the wrong end. Misled by a theory about progress, I assumed that the modernist painters were in every sense an advance on their predecessors. Conventionalism meant death. This, I decided, must also apply to poetry. Some one having told me that my poems were just like those of the Sitwells, I began

to read the Sitwells. Their little jazz fantasies seemed
to me extremely exciting. They were in tune with
the 'child-like' painting of Matisse and the sentimental harlequins of Picasso's blue period.

I liked about the Sitwells their 'difficulty', their
Russian Ballet colouring, their pose as 'enfants ter-
ribles'. I liked their child-cult because I was afraid
of growing up and their contempt for public-school
values because I wanted to grow up out of school.
I liked their rococo ornament, their gallery of fantastic figures (at this time I was re-reading all my
fairy-stories). I liked their surprise effects, their
transference of sense-epithets:

> Jane, Jane,
> Tall as a crane,
> The morning light creaks down again.

Though here they were only using, though much
more frequently, a trick of ordinary speech. For
example, the word 'harsh', which properly belongs
to the objects of touch, has been transferred also to
sounds, tastes, and colours.

'Straight' poetry began to bore me—unless it was
ballads or love-poetry. And from the ballads I would
isolate stanzas to use as incantation:

> O rowe my lady in satin and silk
> And wash my son in the morning milk.

I took to the poetry of conceits, to Marvell's 'Apple-
ton House', though I still reserved Shelley for orgi-
astic or missionary moments. Literature had become
miles removed from life. My life, at home or at
school, was so inadequate to my emotional demands
that I fled towards euphuism on the one hand and a

dream-world on the other. For a couple of years I was to respond almost hypnotically to mention of a peacock's tail or a pearl dissolved in wine, or to certain mythological allusions—the mere names Ganymede or Circe.

At this time (1925) I wrote a paper for a school society attacking 'Common Sense' and, incidentally, Science and the Royal Academy. It began with a little parable glorifying a madman who 'published a book of poems which were so good that he was not allowed to be buried in consecrated ground. Such gentlemen were Spenser, Hans Andersen, Apuleius, Mr. Lear—and, in fact, nearly all great writers.'

I had learned well the lesson of post-War Anti-Reason, for I go on, 'Common Sense is like Jargon: it can only say a thing in one way. Sense is good prose and Nonsense is poetry.'

And having quoted the nursery rhyme:

> Wooley Foster has a hen,
> Cockle button, cockle ben,
> She lays eggs for gentlemen,
> But none for Wooley Foster—

I explain 'Wooley Foster is the scientist and nature his hen'.

I then quote from the 'Bacchae' of Euripides—'Thou must be warned, father, even thou and I, not to have pleasure in base logicalities', and go on to defend the Sitwells, saying that their matter is old—the traditional matter of poetry—but that their manner is new and necessarily so. 'Facts are the foundation of everything but for most people they have to be touched up to mean anything.'

I then make a criticism with which I should still agree:

'Edith Sitwell has been said to owe a great deal to the sound of her words but I think that associations are greatly responsible for her fascination. This can be seen in her names. There are some names like Babylon that can never be dissociated from a certain atmosphere. Queen Anne always carries her atmosphere. And even original names like Miss Pekoe cannot be summed up as so much sound value. Our minds are too quick for our ears.'

Having defended fantasy-poetry, I then add quickly:

'But you must not think that good things are only to be found in Xanadu or in past history. The dwellers in Xanadu never saw a van going down the street and piled with petrol tins in beautiful reds and yellows and greens. . . . This age is as *romantically interesting* [italics later] as any other age . . . and science is really an advantage; it is the narrowly scientific spirit, the common sense spirit, the reduction of everything to formulae, that is the fly in the ointment.'

About four months later I wrote another paper, also on the road to surrealism but now admitting that 'Romance' (still the supreme quality) 'is everywhere, even in the mind of the mathematician'.

Into this paper I inserted a defence of the ballad:

'The ballad is childlike too because of its simple and narrow plots. There is little individualism here. Children are conventionalists. Yet again there is the appeal to children in its tragedy. My earliest memory is one of memories and they were melancholy. Ballads are usually melancholy. There is the regret for the lost wonderland; the wonderland offered and then disproved in the cold light of sophistication;

"O haud your tongue o' weeping" he says,
 "Let a' your follies a-bee;
I'll show you where the white lilies grow
 On the banks o' Italie."

But he is lying or rather joking—

 "O haud your tongue, my dearest dear,
  Let a' your follies a-bee,
 I'll show you where the white lilies grow
  In the bottom o' the sea." '

After a gibe at Wordsworth I come back to 'Romance' as the birthright of children:

'When I was little I lived in a perpetual chiaroscuro; noises ticked themselves into other noises, the cracks on the ceiling slid into faces and the marble markings on the mantel-piece became an epic with a hundred plots. Mowing-machines reappeared in dreams to chase me; they lived in the hen-house; without drums were beating and soldiers marched about, very stiff and wooden and red. Romantic poetry is the stuff of personal dreams made sufficiently impersonal to be palatable to others than oneself.'

And giving as an 'example of the irrelevances of the Romanticist' the nursery rhyme 'Hush-a-by, baby, on the tree-top', I explain 'The romanticist will not be in a position to judge of the intrinsic merits of this. It will be to him a symbol . . . he will turn it from one picture into many better ones', and I argue that this poem, for example, could easily and legitimately expand into the legend of Diana and Endymion. [I suspect that at this time I had been reading Robert Graves's *Poetic Unreason*.]

After which I rise to a surrealist enthusiasm— 'The business of the poets is to produce rabbits out of apparent vacancy. . . . They supply the missing pieces to our jigsaws. They delve into our brains and fish up the king of the salmon from beneath the weeds of convention.' [It is always assumed that conventions are weeds.]

I end the paper by quoting Yeats's 'Happy Town-land', the 'Pervigilium Veneris', and Theocritus' re-frain:

ἴϋγξ ἕλκε τὺ τῆνον ἐμὸν ποτὶ δῶμα τὸν ἄνδρα

with the typical 'romantic' comment—'She may chant on, she may mix her philtres, he will never come.' Still self-pity, the child-cult, the sacrificing of thought to music and colour.

This attitude survived till I left school. In my last term at Marlborough I wrote a paper with the ironic title 'Fool, Put Childish Things Away', which be-gins: 'One must put away childish things, I suppose, but why so early?' This paper is a hotch-potch of the 'Song of Songs', Lord Dunsany, and the 'Golden Ass' of Apuleius. I was feeling sentimental about leaving school.

During my last two years at school, then, I had been reading poetry either for its fantastic qualities (as the Sitwells), or its sensuous qualities (as Keats), or its anarchist rebelliousness (as Shelley), or its open sexiness (as Marlowe's 'Hero and Leander'). In the midst of this, at the age of 18, I met the poems of Eliot, which I found repellent. His subject-matter was ugly, I did not like his form, and I found him very obscure. But I went on reading him because I had read somewhere that he was the best of the modern poets. After a time I was able to squeeze him into my fantasy world. I had always had a taste for nightmare as well as for the dreams of wish-fulfilment and here were patches of genuine nightmare relieving the drab realism:

The moon has lost her memory.
A washed-out smallpox cracks her face,
Her hand twists a paper rose,
That smells of dust and eau de Cologne . . .

or

A woman drew her long black hair out tight
And fiddled whisper music on those strings
And bats with baby faces in the violet light
Whistled, and beat their wings
And crawled head downward down a blackened wall
And upside down in air were towers
Tolling reminiscent bells, that kept the hours
And voices singing out of empty cisterns and exhausted wells.

And soon I began to like Eliot's contemporary content. Hitherto I had looked on the contemporary world as containing properties—like the brightly coloured petrol tins mentioned above—which could be abstracted from it merely for the sake of *décor* or else as providing people—types—who could serve as butts (like Osbert Sitwell's General). There was plenty of such obvious satire in Eliot and I took readily to his cheaper poems such as 'Aunt Helen' and 'The Hippopotamus', but there were other poems where common or squalid objects took on a massiveness unobtainable in the thin cartoons of the pure satirist. Here the two moments were simultaneously present which Eliot himself has called the 'boredom and the glory' of daily existence.

Further, as I had for some time been converting my sexual feelings into a kind of museum or puppet-show, it made me feel very adult to read in 'The Waste Land', the account of the seduction of the typist:

> On the divan are piled (at night her bed)
> Stockings, slippers, camisoles, and stays. . . .

Such 'realism' seemed to me then more real than it does now because I contrasted it with Circe, Keats, Hero and Leander.

And, when I had discovered its principles, I admired Eliot's technique—the blend of conversation and incantation, the deliberate flatnesses, the quick cutting, the so-called free association. I had already been advocating such an approach in the papers above quoted and a year before in my long poem I had attempted deliberately to write flatly when describing everyday sordid properties:

> within it is empty
> Like a loft and a small boy sits
> On a petrol can with his bare feet covered
> In a heap of cigarette ends and adulterate straws.

[But notice the romantic epithet 'adulterate'.] 'Truth' rather than 'Beauty' was now my guiding concept, though my truth was falsified by the individualist pessimism so common among modern adolescents.

I took Eliot's poems to the O.T.C. camp and read them in a stuffy canteen while smoking forbidden cigarettes, and when the book got smeared with cigarette ash I was pleased, feeling it appropriate. Since then my view of Eliot has balanced itself, but

I still think of the earlier Eliot as the poet of cigarette stubs—not a great poet nor essentially a tragic poet, but a very sensitive aesthete in literature, learned in and obsessed with the past, for whom the problem is not the problem of a world-builder or a believer or a rebel or even a reporter, but the problem of a rather pedantic individualist who would like his daily life and his personal relationships to conform to some pattern which he has extracted from other people's poetry or philosophy. But that conformity is un-achievable and so he sits blowing smoke-rings.

ii

My first feeling on leaving school was that I was free not only to write poetry but to live poetically. (I still thought of the poet as a madman who could not be buried in consecrated ground. I must escape from the Church of Ireland and the playing-fields of Marlborough.) With a careful cynicism I depreciated Oxford even before I went up. But I hoped to talk a lot there, to drink, and to study 'Significant Form'. I should not attempt to be a hero, for the ineffectual young men in Tchekov were preferable to all the heroes of Shakespeare. Talk was preferable to action (a revival of my Irish nationalist feelings reminded me that I belonged to a nation of talkers). Images and rhythm were the most important things in the world.

It had not occurred to me that the theory of Significant Form, which I took from Clive Bell, is a contradiction in terms. In any object, poem or picture, which shows 'significant form', according to this

theory, the shape is valuable *for the shape's own sake.*
But 'significant', on any analysis, ought to mean
significant of something outside itself.

Inconsistently with this theory I was eager for
new sensations. I had not yet read D. H. Lawrence,
but, when I was not thinking of the creative faculty
as a pure instinct for shape, I was thinking of it as
a syndicate of guts and senses. Self-Expression was
an alternative to Significant Form. And Self-Expression meant the expression of certain egotistical moods
—for example, nostalgia for childhood, Wanderlust,
terror of the unknown, melancholy at the passing of
time, and (probably underlying all these) the frus-
trated sex desires of a young man who was a virgin.
Witness the following poem written before I went to
Oxford:

> The sea, now hoary with desire,
> Yet follows feet that walk the beach;
> The sensual plumes of brine aspire
> But cannot reach beyond their reach—
> Will amour'd Neptune never tire?

Note the conventional poetic diction, the pose, the
tricked-out or 'sublimated' sexuality.

And I continued to dwell on my old text—that
growing up is a spiritual deterioration, writing, for
example:

> When I was small, each tree was voluble,
> Each shrubbery Dodona. . . .

which was exactly in the same key as much of Edith
Sitwell's 'Troy Park':

But Dagobert and Peregrine and I [= Osbert and Sacheverell
    and I]
Were children then; we walked like shy gazelles
Among the music of the thin flower-bells.
And life still held some promise,—never ask
Of what,—but life seemed less a stranger, then,
Than ever after in this cold existence.
I always was a little outside life. . . .

Requiring all mood and no argument, I failed to
give my poems an organic unity. They rambled from
image to image and from phrase to phrase. I made
little alteration in a poem after writing it and sometimes the writing was almost automatic. I attempted
to dope my mind and see what would come out of it.
I went up to Oxford with a belief in blind inspiration (similar to that held by even academic authori-
ties such as the Abbé Brémond or A. E. Housman).

IV

MY CASE-BOOK: OXFORD

For me, when I went to Oxford, anything was of interest and therefore nothing was of interest. Anything might serve equally well as material for me to put form upon; consequently my form suffered because the material itself ought to affect the form, but, to be able to do that, the material must be allowed to have rights of its own. The material of literature, more than that of the other arts, is instinct with meaning to start with. For the material of literature is the lives, thoughts, and feelings of men. I had no system which could at the same time unify the world and differentiate its parts significantly. I had no world-view (and any such view is implicitly moral) which could give me a hierarchy, however approximate, of good and evil. The most that I attained to was a vague epicureanism.

The good poet has a definite attitude to life; most good poets, I fancy, have more than that—they have beliefs (though their beliefs need not be *explicit* in their work). A poem is a concrete of form and matter, two moments which the critic in analysis abstracts and separates, but which cannot be divorced in practice. The material of poetry is largely 'enformed' to start with, for the thoughts of men have a definite shape, even before the poet rearranges them, and their feelings have a distinctive quality. Conversely, the form of poetry includes far more than the surface

patterns of rhythm or sentence-structure; it is also
the juxtaposition of images and the balance of idea
against idea.

When I went up to Oxford I felt hampered by this
lack of belief or system and in my first term there
(1926) I wrote a paper which was a partial recanta-
tion of the doctrines expressed in my school-papers.
Having deplored contemporary scepticism (as represented by Aldous Huxley) and complained that our
modern cynics 'have none of Lucretius' frenzy of
disbelief', I advocate a 'return to seriousness'. But
seriousness still seems to mean the practice of art.
(About this time I read with enthusiasm Havelock
Ellis's *The Dance of Life*.) However, I have already
turned against Clive Bell 'who is a great snob towards
what he calls life. . . . "To appreciate a work of art,"
he says, "we need bring with us nothing from life,
no knowledge of its ideas and affairs, no familiarity
with its emotions." This last sentence seems to me
pitiably silly. . . . To me it seems that art is a restatement of life in a purified (or, if you like, in a sublimated) form. . . . I believe firmly in genuine
mystics, but I also believe firmly that art is distinct
from mysticism. . . .' And I go on to renounce
another of my masters in Robert Graves, criticizing
his exaltation of the Unconscious in his book *Poetic
Unreason* together with Plato's doctrine of Poetic
Madness in the *Ion*. 'I do not think it really necessary to shift one's burden on to the void in this way.
. . . The Unconscious has, I suppose, a certain share
in every poem, but why the conscious should therefore retreat altogether before it, I cannot see. The

Unconscious is only the storehouse of what was conscious once and will be conscious again.' I go on to say that 'we should exploit our self-consciousness and not fall into trances of automatic writing. To be thoroughly conscious of oneself is very difficult, and this is, I think, the first reason why men write poetry. It is to introduce myself to me.' Note here the stress on *self*-consciousness. I believed at that time, or thought I believed, that there was no such thing as altruism. Metaphysically, I was very near solipsism.

Then, on the metaphysical ground that all plurality is make-believe anyway, I write:

'If you must write poetry, don't decline the charge of artificiality. It is only a further link in a chain of artifices—Life, men, society, language. The more the sounder. Lie often enough and your lies will be truth.

'The body is necessary for the soul. As our soul has become more complex (and has become human from bestial) it has had to extend its body, to overflow and find release in a supplementary body of language. In language here I include all the arts. . . . A poem is a sort of supplementary body that allows us communion with ourselves. . . . The business of the poetic body is to exteriorise a sample of oneself and incidentally of humanity. Now there is ready to us a vast corpus of poetry which I might think sufficient to my needs without me producing any of my own. This is wrong. Such poetry is a sample of humanity, only incidentally of myself.'

I go on to defend poetic conventions: 'I believe that any convention or artifice whatsoever must when applied to any material whatsoever produce something new and that the use of, e.g. rhyme will probably elevate a statement which is already intelligible and even obvious as prose.' The convention can even take the lead, and I quote, as an example of 'rhyme taking the lead without leading the sense to irrelevance or insincerity', Blake's poem:

> Merry, merry sparrow!
> Under leaves so green,
> A happy blossom
> Sees you, swift as arrow,
> Seek your cradle narrow
> Near my bosom.
>
> Pretty, pretty robin!
> Under leaves so green,
> A happy blossom
> Hears you sobbing, sobbing,
> Pretty, pretty robin,
> Near my bosom.

After which I say that not all conventions are always suitable—'the heroic couplet as used by Pope would now be a bad convention if used by a contemporary poet and could be justly damned as conventional'—but that poetry always requires *some* conventions.

'The prevalence of strange symptoms such as *vers libre* does not imply anarchy. Anarchy is the death of poetry. If such poems are not dead they must be conforming to some order which we do not immediately notice. We must therefore think what conventions are being used by poets to-day as proper to the circumstances of to-day. . . .

'The super-convention in all ages is to be traditional. This implies constant change and probably frequent revolution. As Mr. T. S. Eliot says: "To conform merely would be for the new work not really to conform at all."'

I then discuss literary influences: 'To accuse a poet of being derivative is mere silliness, as he obviously is derivative'—and quote Eliot again: 'No poet, no artist of any art, has his complete meaning alone. His significance, his appreciation is the appreciation of his relation to the dead poets and artists. [Note *dead*; and note *poets* and *artists*.] You cannot value him alone: you must set him, for contrast and comparison, among the dead. I mean this as a principle of aesthetic, not merely historical, criticism.'

Having tried, not very successfully, to analyse in Eliot's own poetry 'both the traditionalism and the novelty', I dissect the contemporary literary scene and attack 'Verisimilitude':

'So-called natural art seems to be attempting the impossible, i.e. trying to achieve in the medium of paint or words or marble what has been achieved to perfection in the medium of flesh or chlorophyll and is only in that medium achieveable. . . . We understand that all art is theatrical and that the success of the piece depends not on an accurate likeness to anything off the stage but on a self-contained coherence upon it (which artificial coherence naturally corresponds to some desire or potentiality in nature previously unsatisfied).'

And, defending both, I compare the present period to the Alexandrian; such a period is 'not the result of individual decadence, but the inevitable next stage in the stream of literature. . . . "Speech", says Shelley, "created thought." Therefore, if you disbelieve in thought and can yet express your disbelief in words, you have gloriously confuted yourself and created a world out of nothing.' I give as examples Eliot and Joyce; I saw so much disbelief expressed in contemporary literature that I had to posit thus a creed *of words*. 'Speech creating thought' was my text most of the time I was at Oxford.

Two years later I wrote a fantasy-paper which showed no advance on this, advocating garrulity with a text from Falstaff: 'I have a whole school of tongues in this belly of mine.' I had now read some philosophy and was more sceptical than ever about objective values. I invent a little parable, the hero of which declares that 'Art is the Gift of the Gab'. I subscribe to Nietzsche's eulogy of 'Dionysianism' in 'The Birth of Tragedy', and, when once more attacking the 'academicians', preach that there is a great need in the modern world for humour—blasphemy, obscenity, parody, caricature. As an example of 'cathartic' contrast I quote a poem by W. H. Auden (1928):

> In Spring we waited. Princes felt
>   Through darkness for unwoken queens;
> The itching lover weighed himself
>   At stations on august machines. . . .

I then fall foul of Schopenhauer for maintaining (in my words):

'that art was the abnegation, the only possible one, of the will and that therefore it was so admirable because in art alone we could find an escape from the wheel of will-work and the throbs and jangle of existence. Art was non-existence made up into pills and packets, a short cut to Nirvana, a temporary suicide, easily available for the afternoon and much less painful. . . . This is a view which I entirely disagree with. Art is essentially an expression, not necessarily of *joie de vivre*, but at any rate of the lust of living. . . .' This is true, I claim, even of such 'suicidal' poetry as Webster's or Eliot's. 'The very act of saying how they feel means that they have not yet abnegated feeling. . . . When Cleopatra advocates suicide . . . her very desire for suicide signifies a masterly appreciation of life.'

In an earlier paper (1927) on Joyce's *Ulysses* I took the one-sided view that *Ulysses* is primarily a sinister or tragic work. At that time I was unnaturally, because inhumanly, opposed to every symptom of industrial or commercial vulgarity and speak unashamedly of 'Mr. Bloom's horrible home'. For Mr. Bloom himself, that sympathetic figure, I have no good words at all. But I pompously advocate that 'our way of escape is . . . to reintroduce the phallos to religion and religion to the phallos'. And I quote the following bad lines from Harold Monro as giving a true picture of the cold Zeitgeist to which the phallos must be opposed:

> Two battleships for feet,
> Two Eiffel Towers for legs, for your thin arms
> Two cranes that either lift ten thousand tons;
> Your ribs long spans of bridges, your cold heart
> Big Ben; your liver clogged with bile, your guts infirm,
> Cluttered with refuse; your large, belching stomach
> Bulging with factories you have gulpingly swallowed
> All regulated by your clockwork heart.
> But when at last I come to try your face,
> I can see nothing.

After which I quote, as an example of the pseudo-romanticism which is complementary to this grim industrialism, an advertisement of George Lunn's 'Tours in Spain'. From such garish clichés, I say, we must get back to the human reality which is a concrete of soul and sex, and I quote with approval Hugh M'Diarmid:

> Man's spreit is wi' his ingangs twined
> In ways that we can ne'er unwind

and repeat D. H. Lawrence's remarks on 'the absolute reality of the sensuous experience'. Lawrence's cult of the blood and senses was now tending to take the place of my child-cult, though I was rather damped by Wyndham Lewis's attack on both in the first number of *The Enemy* (January 1927).

My evolution during this period was typical, I think, of that of many contemporary undergraduates at Oxford and Cambridge. My ideology was built up on *Ulysses*, 'The Waste Land', and the novels of D. H. Lawrence. As the two former are essentially negative works, my positive creed was inevitably Lawrentian. But, as I was not an initiate into the practical workings of this creed, I was always open to a charge either of insincerity or ignorance. Christopher Isherwood's autobiographical book, *Lions and Shadows*, shows how at Cambridge at about the same time two young men, who have since become realistic writers with political interests, spent their intellectual energy on a fantastic nursery make-believe.

I spent my last two years at Oxford reading philosophy (mainly idealist metaphysics). I also read Wyndham Lewis's attacks on the leading modernist writers, subsequently published in *Time and Western Man*. Influenced by these eristic writings I wrote in my last year at Oxford (1930) a paper entitled 'We are the Old' (a phrase taken from Gentile's 'Mind as Pure Act'):

'Revolt, freedom and self-expression—these are the most unoriginal things in the world.... The volcano is not the archetype of artistic activity. . . . Self-expression is a resuscitation of Plato's theory in the Ion, the poet as mere vehicle. . . . Platonic inspiration and modern self-expression are both alike a renunciation of our human birthright, the right of living on the surface. . . . The poets [in Plato] are always κατεχόμενοι, never ἔμφρονες. "For a poet," says Plato, "is an unsubstantial thing, winged and holy, and he cannot do anything till he is inspired and frenzied and no longer in possession of his wits."

'This heresy greatly influenced Shelley, who writes, "When composition begins, inspiration is already on the decline, and the most glorious poetry that has ever been communicated to the world is probably a feeble shadow of the original conception of the poet." With this I disagree. The opposition of composition to inspiration may be valid, but, if so, poetry must necessarily fall on the side of composition. . . .

'Croce again seems to support the Ion heresy by ante-dating the *poietic* act, by allowing the artistic activity its consummation before the production of a work of art. . . .

'The difference between error and truth is a difference of degree. Human error invariably hits a mark of some sort and human knowledge invariably misses the bull's eye. There are two frequent distortions of this obvious statement. There is the self-assertive, euphemistic distortion of some modern poets and painters who claim that any blot or burbling is art because it is not nothing, and there is that of morbid religionists—the truth is not in us.'

I go on to argue that truth must always have an element of novelty:

'That Queen Anne is dead was once true and so (speaking absolutely) is true for ever. But one of the principles of living on the surface is never to speak absolutely. For truth ossifies into truism and a truism (speaking relatively) is a falsity. . . .

'This is where a knowledge of tradition is so important. We can't know our present tense until we know our past. Let us leave sincerity out of it. . . . We must distinguish sincerity and truth. Sincerity belongs to the individual. Truth belongs to the generation. So that people who write love-songs in the Elizabethan or Romantic or Victorian manner may be completely sincere, they may be even adequately "expressing themselves", they may get the real artist's thrill when they rhyme flowers with hours or when they string together beautiful words like topaz turquoise malachite. They are sincere but they are also untrue. . . . We can only find truth in novelty.'

I then express sympathy with William James's 'reluctance to put the flux through the mangle' and argue that E. E. Cummings's 'insistence on poetry not as something made but as making is a mere corollary of or implicate in Gentile's main thesis that knowledge is not things thought but thinking'.

But, on the other hand, I attack the literary doctrine of the Chunk of Life: 'Art is essentially artificial. You are, to start with, irretrievably artificial when you set pen to paper, when you select, when you limit a book by beginning or end.' And I attack the two extremes of out-and-out 'realism' and out-and-out 'self-expression': 'Words refuse either to be merely descriptive (slaves of the other) or merely expressive (slaves of the self).' Walt Whitman is an example of a wrong-headed attempt at spontaneity: 'Whitman's titles are significant, the guiding principle of All-ness and secondly the principle of Whitman as an End in Itself—One's Self I Sing; Me Imperturbe; Song of Myself;

I Sing the Body Electric; Spontaneous Me; Salut au Monde;
A Song of the Rolling Earth; Song for All Seas, All Ships;
O Me! O Life! . . .

"I sing the Universal", says Whitman, and accordingly forgets the art of living on the surface, the art of limit. . . . He
is all for affirming everything, he forgets to negate:

I have heard what the talkers were talking, the talk of the
    beginning and the end
But I do not talk of the beginning or the end.
There was never any more inception than there is now
Nor any more youth or age than there is now
And will never be any more perfection than there is now,
Nor any more heaven and hell than there is now.
Urge and urge and urge
Always the procreant urge of the world.

'Here,' I comment, 'Walt Whitman convicts himself out
of his own mouth. Writing is itself entirely a matter of beginning or ending. . . . He says "I do not talk of the beginning or
the end" and proceeds to write poetry. The illogicality is
parallel to "Woodbine Willie's" title to a book of poems—
The Unutterable Beauty. . . .

'In the same section of "Song of Myself", Whitman says:

"To elaborate is no avail, learned and unlearned feel that it
    is so."

and then

"Clear and sweet is my soul, and clear and sweet is all that is
    not my soul."

'This is "democracy" in the worst sense. Poetry is essentially
oligarchic, even snobbish. To put the unlearned on the same
level as the learned, i.e. to reduce both to the level of mere
feeling where no elaboration is required, is to assert the vague
profundity which is their identity and to neglect their essential surface distinctions. Whitman was proclaiming the same

heresy that Tolstoy was preaching in Russia in his book *What is Art?*—trying to be simple, genuine, primitive.'

I revert to the necessity for a compromise between spontaneity and artifice, between tradition and experiment:

'An historical sense is essential, which means that we must know how to be *new*, as contrasted with repetition—psittacosis—on the one hand, and with escape from tradition—aphasia—on the other. We must sit in the seats of our ancestors, i.e. we must turn our ancestors out of them.'

I then criticize the psychological approach to poetry:

' "Really to understand Caliban," says Mr. Graves in his book *Poetic Unreason*, "enormously more history has to be discovered, beside which our present knowledge appears negligible." This is a confusion. "Really to understand" a cat we should have to know all its physiology and the whole theory of evolution in general and the whole history of that cat's heredity in particular; but actually we can get as good, or probably a better, idea of cattiness without all that. This is the truth implied in Aristotle's doctrine that art is of the *typical*. Not typical as contrasted with individual, but typical as contrasted with particular.'

I end with two sweeping generalizations:

'Poetry is saying ordinary things in an extraordinary way', and 'An artist's humanity is so great that he is inevitably a misanthrope. This is because humanity, as Aristotle saw, is only realized in what we should call the flower of humanity.'

I went down from Oxford and got married while still holding firmly to these two tenets: (i) that what makes a poem a poem is its artificiality; (ii) that poetry is a pursuit for the few, that these few are the pick of humanity, and that when they speak they speak for themselves rather than for others. These tenets I still consider to be half-truths, but barren ones (my literary evolution described above can be seen as a dialectic of half-truths), and it is not surprising that for about three years after leaving Oxford I almost gave up reading or writing modern poetry.

Marriage at least made me recognize the existence of other people in their own right and not as vicars of my godhead. And I realized that while it is an asset to have an idiom, an idiom is only valuable as a differentiation of what is communal. Further, I had to earn my own living and this is antipathetic to a purely aesthetic view of life. And lastly, living in a large industrial city, Birmingham, I recognized that the squalor of Eliot was a romanticized squalor because treated, on the whole, rather bookishly as *décor*. The 'short square fingers stuffing pipes' were not brute romantic objects abstracted into a picture by Picasso, but were living fingers attached to concrete people—were even, in a sense, *my* fingers.

V

THE PERSONAL FACTOR

ITERARY criticism should always be partly bio-
graphical. For obvious reasons this is difficult
when the critic is discussing his contemporaries.
Even if he knows the facts of their family history
and their finances, their home-lives and love-lives,
he is not at liberty to give most of these facts to the
public. I hold with Freud that most poets are neurotic above the average, though I would not agree
either that they are for this reason unhappy or their
work of little value. But it would be tactless, if not
libellous, in me to try to analyse in detail the particular neuroses of particular living poets. I may mention generally that I have met several poets who had
had strained relations with, if not antagonism towards, one or both of their parents, and several who
were strongly homosexual. These facts obviously
condition their poetry.

It is to be noted that now, as in most periods, the
great majority of poets comes from the middle classes.
Both the very rich and the poor are hampered by
ignorance. The rich do not bother to read and the
poor have not the facilities (a certain amount of reading is usually a necessary preliminary for writing,
though too much reading may make a poet bookish).
But as education comes more within the reach of
the proletariat, it is to be expected that proletarians
will bring new blood to poetry, as is happening in

America. Thus D. H. Lawrence, a miner's son, having acquired enough education to be able to write, was able to write with more verve than most of his contemporaries. He had not inherited the stale thought of a class. But, on the other hand, for the reason that he had moved out of his class, his thought and vision faded. Compare one of his last novels, *The Plumed Serpent*, with the early *Sons and Lovers*.

I doubt if I should have written poetry myself if I had not been the son of a clergyman. Clergymen do not have to fight for money, their salaries being fixed and their vicarages rent-free. Therefore, however poor they are, they are not as liable as many people to be bound by commercial values. Secondly, a child in a clergyman's house usually has a good deal of time to itself. Thirdly, most clergymen have plenty of books in their houses.

The Greek poets are always held up to us as examples of normal human beings, but we do not know enough about them to be sure on this point. In the modern world, at any rate, a surprising number of poets have had obvious psychological complexes and, quite frequently, like Byron or Pope, physical abnormalities. I have noticed among the poets whom I have met that they are often physically clumsy, or short sighted or weedy. As children they have had night-terrors or been bullied. Some were afraid of sex and some were precociously erotic. They grow up to use their poetry as a weapon. It is their way of showing off. This, of course, does not invalidate their poetry any more than a geometrical demonstration is unsound because the geometer shows off in his geometry. Nor does the fact that so many poets start with a kink or deficiency conflict with the principle stated in my first and second chapters, that poetry is a normal activity. For writing poetry is the way that the poet *returns to normal*.

An obvious contemporary example of the vain poet is Yeats, who admits that poetry is a pose. But it is, he insists, a stock pose, approved by history and permanently valid. Most poets have not been so conscious of themselves as poseurs, and I suspect that so extreme and continuous a self-consciousness is hampering to the poet. Any pose, like the poses in ballet-dancing, is a development of something natural. Our muscles have it in them. It is as well then that the muscles (which in the poet's case are his instincts) should have a good deal of say in the postures which he adopts. Poetry tends to fail when it is too *voulu*.

Most good poets have not had it all their own way, i.e. not their own way as they deliberately would choose to have it. There is always a part of them which thinks otherwise or which at least is interested in something that they think merely incidental. Most good poetry therefore is an unconscious collaboration between Jekyll and Hyde.

Jekyll is the poet as he thinks he is or consciously wishes to be. Hyde is his suppressed and subordinate self (or the self which, *as a poet*, he would wish to suppress and subordinate). Hyde complements and corrects Jekyll, sometimes indeed by sabotage.

I would not equate Jekyll and Hyde respectively

with the Conscious and the Unconscious, nor again, say, with the Reason and the Emotions. The equation differs in different poets. Thus in Milton Hyde is the pagan but in Baudelaire Hyde is the Christian. In A. E. Housman Hyde is the Reason and in Euripides Hyde is the Mystic. In T. S. Eliot Hyde is the yogi-man, but in Yeats Hyde is Common Sense. In the Romantics Hyde is the brain; in the Pure Poet Hyde is outside interests. In Virgil Hyde is the individualist who gave the reins to Dido. But A. E. is an example of a poet whose Hyde (in his case the shrewdness he showed in business) never broke into his poetry, which consequently is thin and watery, lacking stiffening.

Compromise is a virtue in the arts, though one that is usually practised unconsciously. I should say that most of the great poets have been compromisers (Patin pointed this out even in the case of Lucretius, who appears at first sight unusually one-minded). Literary criticism's great vice is that it will take any individual poet as a pure specimen of any one tendency or attitude. It would be a more valid method for the critic to try to work out in each poet a kind of Hegelian dialectic of opposites, remembering again to stress the fusion of these opposites rather than their opposition.

I think myself that provided the fusion is successful, poetry will be the richer the greater the conflict resolved in it. Thus Wilfred Owen appears to me a finer poet than Siegfried Sassoon. Sassoon's war-poems are more one-minded, more purely polemical, more pat. One might argue therefore that they were

better as being more closely appropriate to their subject. Owen, like Sassoon, is inspired by disgust and
hatred, but a sort of epic idealism persists which
reveals itself when he writes in the grand manner:

> By choice they made themselves immune
> To pity and whatever mourns in man
> Before the last sea and the hapless stars;
> Whatever mourns when many leave these shores;
> Whatever shares
> The eternal reciprocity of tears.

Owen, as I have said, grew up in readiness to
write like Keats, in which case his poetry might well
have been, in Plato's phrase, 'an imitation of an
imitation', for Keats, at least in his longer works, was
always modelling himself, to his own detriment, on
one of the old masters—say Milton or Spenser. The
War dissolved the Keats in Owen and made him a
far finer poet then he would—probably—otherwise
have been; but it could only make him a poet thanks
to the lesser poet whom it broke in him. His horrors
convince because he is not merely a statistician collecting them; for the sensuous man in him persists:

> And the far valley behind, where the buttercup
> Had blessed with gold their slow boots coming up. . . .

And the grandiose phrase-maker remains alive in
him (it is surprising how traditionally poetic he is in
his imagery and epithets). And the technician, of
course, goes on experimenting (he had tried out his
'pararhymes' before the War, appropriate as these
often are to his war subjects). All these things which
left to themselves might have lost him in decorative

or escapist or merely experimental writing, fused,
under the control of one dominating subject, into
poetry of a very high order. The 'total impression'
demanded by Matthew Arnold rides forward un-
falteringly upon all his tricks and phrases.

A clear example of a poet whose work embodies
conflicting interests is Gerard Manley Hopkins.
Critics have argued that he is a poet in spite of his
Jesuitry, others that he is a poet because of it. I
feel that he might well have written more poetry had
he not been a Jesuit, but that then the gain in quantity would have meant a loss in quality. An eye for
nature by itself is not enough to make a poet (Query:
Did Monet's eye make him a painter?) Perhaps it
is not even enough to have an eye for nature joined
with technical virtuosity in verse-making. Hopkins's
Christian belief is *structurally* essential to his poems,
and I cannot imagine them existing without it. This
is not to deny that the pagan is there in him also.

Of poets living and writing to-day I notice that
Yeats is a federation—more self-conscious than is
usual—of opposing interests (see the passages from
his essays already quoted). In this he resembles his
master, William Morris, that Janus with one face
looking briskly forward to socialism, but the other
face looking wanly (to use his own favourite word)
back to a medieval Never-Never Land. Yeats is a
person of common sense who has taken a not un-
realistic part in Irish politics and in the managing
of a theatre, a hard-headed controversialist, a wit,
a good publicity man, a practical snob. But he is
also, of course, a spiritualist, a hankerer for yoga, a

malingerer in fairyland. The fairy-lover Yeats was for some time dominant, but the experiences of life, coupled with a change of diet in reading (and also, perhaps, a change of diet literally) have for many years now adjusted the balance. Swift and Bishop Berkeley are not for Yeats the Swift and Berkeley of the student of literature and philosophy. They, like Lady Gregory or O'Leary or Rabindranath Tagore, have been roped into his private mythology to join Deirdre and Cuchulain and Mohini Chatterjee. But for all that they have contributed sharpness and drive to his verse.

Yeats's numerous essays and autobiographical writings give the reader plenty of clues to his development. Unhappy as a child, he took to make-believe, a habit easily acquired in the West of Ireland, a country of superstitious peasants and of gentry who lived in the past. He mentions visits to an aunt who had 'a little James the First cream-jug with the Yeats motto and crest'. As a little boy, he says, 'I did not think I could live without religion'. His father had found a religion in art but Yeats has always wavered between this and a home-made religion of his own with a strong flavour of the East. (Though perhaps this only amounts to an art-religion in the end; I suspect that Yeats adopted Indian mysticism to bolster up his thinking and that he wished to bolster up his thinking in order to bolster up his poetry. This suspicion is borne out by his doctrine of the Mask; see Chapter I.)

Going to school in London and convicted as both Irish and unathletic, he found himself to be Yeats

against the world—or against the Anglo-Saxon world
—which role he has proudly sustained ever since:
'To transmute the anti-English passion into a passion of hatred against the vulgarity and materialism
whereon England has founded her worst life and the
whole life that she sends us, has always been a dream
of mine. . . .'

As a boy Yeats went to live in an artistic house in
Bedford Park, decorated in a pre-Raphaelite peacock
blue. A little later, meeting the 'nineties' poets he
acquired a third cause for pride—the pride of the
artist for art's sake, inherited from Pater. This, with
his other two prides—family and national—has given
Yeats that self-assurance without which so esoteric
a poet could hardly have survived.

Yeats's poetry is conditioned by a passion for aris-
tocracy—'Every day I notice some new analogy
between the long-established life of the well-born and
the artist's life. We come from the permanent things
and create them, and instead of old blood we have
old emotions and we carry in our heads always that
form of society aristocracies create now and again
for some brief moment at Urbino or Versailles.' This
aristocratic snobbery has been balanced, or extended,
by Yeats's admiration for the Thersites type, the
beggarly outcast, the ragged rebel, whom he has
taken over from Synge.

I have already quoted Yeats's remarks on the
'relation between discipline and the theatrical sense',
the need to wear a mask. But Yeats's preoccupation
with 'style' and mumming has latterly been modified:
'I now see that the literary element in painting, the

moral element in poetry, are the means whereby the two arts are accepted into the social order and become a part of life and not things of the study and the exhibition.' All that Yeats touches becomes suffused with Yeats, but in those of his later poems which deal with recent events or with people whom he has known, the brute objective quality of such people and events refuses to be mainly submerged in myth:

> I have met them at close of day
> Coming with vivid faces
> From counter or desk among grey
> Eighteenth-century houses.
> I have passed with a nod of the head
> Or polite meaningless words,
> Or have lingered awhile and said
> Polite meaningless words,
> And thought before I had done
> Of a mocking tale or a gibe
> To please a companion
> Around the fire at the club,
> Being certain that they and I
> But lived where motley is worn:
> All changed, changed utterly:
> A terrible beauty is born.

A. E. Housman and D. H. Lawrence were both poets who, like Yeats, tended to impose their discipline from within. Lawrence was a missionary, but an anarchistic, Hyde Park Corner missionary who fled from his own physique and his own social heredity to a South Sea island of exaggerated sexual idealism. Housman, like Rimbaud, after an outburst of rebellious poetry—the rebellion of a lonely individual—turned his back on a medium which involved so much contact with humanity and took to living on his brain in the arid Abyssinia of textual commentary. Housman has left no followers, but Lawrence's enthusiasm has, as I said, been divorced from his anarchy and taken over by younger poets into a more positive synthesis.

Eliot, in a sense less esoteric than Yeats (because he distrusts voodoo and home-made eclectic creeds) is in a sense more esoteric in that he will not commit himself; and the world cannot understand people who will not commit themselves. Eliot has repeatedly been called 'classical', largely on the strength of his own criticism and his own well-known catchword of 'impersonality'. I should not myself call Eliot either classical or impersonal. His economy of statement and precision of image may be 'classical', but not the mood, not the total effect. Nostalgia and self-pity are strong in him if under disguise, and also, under disguise, a certain swagger. And though the image may be less traditionally poetic, the lobster in Prufrock serves the same purpose as the Nightingale in Keats—a symbol of escape from the struggle, of the great refusal:

> I should have been a pair of ragged claws
> Scuttling across the floors of silent seas.

Eliot and his early model, Pound, are both first and foremost American tourists. They wish to shake off the vulgarity of America—of Sweeney, Miss Nancy Ellicott, Mr. Hecatomb Styrax, to become European, cosmopolitan. They take long trips through history and the history of art and literature, eagerly 'aware that the mind of Europe . . . is a mind which changes, and that this change is a development which abandons nothing *en route*, which does not super-annuate either Shakespeare, or Homer, or the rock drawing of the Magdalenian draughtsmen'.

Eliot is a better poet than Pound because in Eliot the dialectic is more exacting; he is not merely a globe-trotter, a dilettante. He looks at ancient elegance and modern vulgarity, but records them rather as a moralist or half-mystic than as a cinematograph machine. It is Eliot's Christian morality (his morality, I think, rather than his creed) that gives drive to his poems. His family were New England puritans. His grandfather, a clergyman, published a sermon on 'Suffering Considered as Discipline'. His mother wrote a dramatic poem on the life of Savonarola. With these precedents he went to Harvard and met a corrective in the humanism of Irving Babbitt and Santayana. Later he took courses at the Sorbonne and Oxford; he studied metaphysics and Sanskrit, read Indian philosophy and F. H. Bradley (*and*, of course, Sir James Frazer), became a successful blend of the don and prophet.

The two younger poets whom I know well, Auden and Spender, are both products of the English professional classes—Auden the son of a doctor, Spender the son of a Liberal politician; Auden went to a public school, Spender did not. Auden spent several years as a schoolmaster, and his general interest in boys' schools has had a huge influence on his poetry. This school background has given him a whole new crop of properties peculiarly suited to a poet whose moral is growth and progress. Like Wordsworth, he brought into poetry a subject-matter considered alien to it by his elders, who would have thought brothels or champagne poetic but not changing-rooms or playing-fields. Auden, who sees the adult in the child and the child in the adult, had the good sense to write about what he was acquainted with. And for this he had the sanction of his favourite psychologists —*maxima debetur puero reverentia*—and the sanction of the sociologists, adolescent youth being the cockpit for striving ideologies.

Auden's father is a doctor especially interested in psychology, but also in Ancient Greece and Rome and in the Icelandic sagas. Auden at Oxford read books of psychology, science, and ethnology when other undergraduates were reading belles-lettres. Going to Germany soon after leaving Oxford, he took readily to post-War Germany's intellectual curiosity and spirit of heroic or idyllic *Kameradschaft*. Returning to England he worked as a schoolmaster and on G.P.O. films. He admires the cinema's unrivalled capacity for rapportage; Auden has always believed that a good writer must be first a good reporter. His poetry is obviously conditioned by his background and experiences, and also by his not unfriendly contempt for the female sex, whom he regards as still precluded from civilization by circumstances.

Spender has in many respects the same background as Auden—a middle-class home life, Oxford, Germany—but being more introverted, more of a sensitive plant, and not having been to a public school, shyer, less inquisitive about his fellows and lacking a sense of humour, has developed a very different type of poetry, less healthy, more consciously poetic, still smacking of the Romantic Revival. The age has made him critical, but his criticism is extremely egotistical and missionary (the two things often go together). He might be regarded as a more economical and self-critical Shelley (like Shelley's his poetry is essentially spiritual; there is little vulgar earth in it).

Compare Shelley:

> The good and mighty of departed ages
>   Are in their graves, the innocent and free,
> Heroes and Poets and prevailing Sages,
>   Who leave the vesture of their majesty
>   To adorn and clothe this naked world. . . .

with Spender:

> The names of those who in their lives fought for life
> Who wore at their hearts the fire's centre.
> Born of the sun they travelled a short while towards the sun
> And left the vivid air signed with their honour.

Mood and attitude are the same in both, though Spender's lines are technically the better.

Neither Spender nor Auden, however, is egocentric when compared with epicurean or dilettante poets like Housman and Pound. Epicureanism, being egocentric, lacks tension. Auden's admiration for the objective world is founded on that cosmic pride which, as distinct from personal pride, lies at the base of Christianity. (He holds that Christianity should be taken up into Communism.) Hence his belief, frivolously expressed, that 'Pelmanism' is an important factor both in art and in the good life. The Epicurean, like the Artist for Art's sake, will have no use for pelmanism. Why burden his mind with facts *which cannot affect his own life*? The Epicurean does not appreciate Otherness as such.

Spender, too, has remarked in conversation that he believes in 'touchability'. Touchability is, on the emotional or physical plane, the counterpart of Auden's pelmanism on the intellectual. It means the renunciation of the utilitarian Epicurean self and the belief that people in themselves and for themselves are worth knowing and touching, just as for Auden facts are worth remembering. A poet like Spender, if he writes a love-poem, will not treat his beloved as a piece of temporary furniture. Spender thinks of himself, to adapt a suggestion of Thomas Mann, as a Marxist who has read Friedrich Hölderlin—i.e. as some one who while recognizing the economic scheme of history and holding the Marxist doctrine of progress can fuse this with his own individual life in the emotions.

Speaking for myself I should say that the following things, among others, had conditioned my poetry —having been brought up in the North of Ireland, having a father who was a clergyman; the fact that my mother died when I was little; repression from the age of 6 to 9; inferiority complex on grounds of physique and class-consciousness; lack of a social life until I was grown up; late puberty; ignorance of music (which could have been a substitute for poetry); inability to ride horses or practise successfully most of the sports which satisfy a sense of rhythm; an adolescent liking for the role of 'enfant terrible'; shyness in the company of young women until I was 20; a liking (now dead) for metaphysics; marriage and divorce; Birmingham; an indolent pleasure in gardens and wild landscapes (Auden, for example, dislikes flowers and prefers landscapes full of the traces of humanity); a liking for animals, an interest in dress.

However much is known about the poet, the poem remains a thing distinct from him. But poetry being firstly communication, a certain knowledge of the poet's personal background will help us to understand him, for his language is to some extent personal. It may be true that any contemporary poet is a mouthpiece of the Zeitgeist, but, as mouthpieces alter what you put into them, it is helpful to consider the shape of the mouthpiece itself. I have no patience with those determinist critics whose determinism merely takes account of *general* conditions—a period in social history, a movement in literary history, or the economic factors in their purity; just as I have no patience with the critic who bases his whole explanation on a poet's psychological biography. Psychology and economics must both be taken into account. We have not reached a stage where one can be subsumed under the other.

VI

IMAGERY

ENGLISH poetry has been notable, at times notorious, for its wealth of imagery. As the famous obscurity of contemporary poets is largely due to their use of imagery, it will be helpful to consider their precedents.

It is a mistake to think of a poet's image as merely an embellishment. Some images, indeed, appear to have been tacked on to the poem from outside, superfluous to the *meaning* of the poem. But often the image, as in Dante, is there to clarify or ram home the meaning. And, again, in many poems (the Symbolists made this into a principle) imagery and meaning are so wedded that they cannot be disintricated. Thus it is possible for the images in a lyric poem to correspond to the characters in a play, the characters in a good play being only separable from its plot or theme by what Aristotle called 'bastard reasoning'.

Aristotle himself in his 'Poetics' uses this bastard reasoning freely, often discussing the formal elements as if they were something added to, instead of something fused with, the subject. While discussing form he states that a poet's most important asset is the gift of metaphor. τὸ γὰρ εὖ μεταφέρειν τὸ τὸ ὅμοιον θεωρεῖν ἐστιν. 'A good metaphor implies an intuitive perception of the similarity in dissimilars.' (Bywater's rather expanded translation.) In agreeing with this

we should remember that, when a poet compares
two things, he does not, necessarily, completely subordinate one to the other. If I say my love is like
a rose, it implies that I also appreciate roses. The
poet, unlike the scientist, is not completely concerned
with his immediate or nominal (what the psychologists call his manifest) subject. When Sir James
Jeans uses a figure, say, of ping-pong balls to explain
astronomical movements, neither his emotions nor
his intellectual curiosity is really concerned with the
ping-pong balls. But the poet's subject tends to
spread beyond its nominal limits. Some poets work
more on the model of the scientist, but none can, or
need, attain to his single-mindedness. (Or, rather,
the poet's single-mindedness is something different
from the scientist's.)

If, then, we draw a distinction between the properties and the images of a poem, this distinction needs
qualifying. The properties are the objects which
enter a poem by their own right, as flowers enter a
poem about a garden, whereas the images enter
a poem by the right of analogy, as flowers entered
Plato's descriptions of his mystical and abstract
Heaven. But, conversely, the properties themselves
may be, in the ultimate analysis, only symbols. Was,
for example, Wordsworth's celandine really all celandine and nothing but celandine?

The form of *simile*, in particular, suggests a subor-
dination of image to property (an approximation,
though usually only a distant one, to the astronomer's
ping-pong balls). The early Chinese poets, in order
to avoid the disintegrating and sometimes falsifying

effects of simile, used a trick which may be called parataxis:

> Tossed is that cypress boat,
> Wave-tossed it floats;
> My heart is in turmoil, I cannot sleep.

The poet is speaking of his heart, but the boat gets a square deal.

We may roughly distinguish the kind of image which is cerebral or 'metaphysical' from the kind of image which is more emotional or physical or intuitive—the former kind coming more from the Reason, the latter rather from the senses or even the Unconscious. (The image given by the senses may, of course, be approved by the Reason, but will appear to be spontaneous rather than contrived; for example, if the stars *looked* like ping-pong balls as well as having movements mathematically corresponding to their movements, the ping-pong-ball image would be both kinds of image simultaneously. Again, the cerebral image, though not given in emotion or intuited in experience, may, of course, be used to *express* emotion.)

Examples will make clearer these distinctions. A cerebral image from Donne:

> If they be two, they are two so
> As stiffe twin compasses are two,
> Thy soule the fixt foot; makes no show
> To move but doth, if th' other do.

A typically vague emotional image from Shelley:

> unimaginable shapes
> Such as ghosts dream dwell in the lampless deep.

A more concrete intuitive image of the dream-type from Blake:

> Helpless, naked, piping loud
> Like a fiend hid in a cloud.

A physical (yet cerebrally correct) image from an early lyric:

> He cam also stille
>   To his modere's bour,
> As dew in Aprille
>   That falleth on the flour.

Many images, as I have said, can be equally cerebral and emotional or physical, nor is the poet's creative process a sure criterion for their distinction. A poet may puzzle out some algebraic symbol for his meaning, which symbol may itself have such a strong physical quality as to dominate the naked meaning. And the poet may even, unconsciously, have been looking for the image for its own sake rather than as an algebraic symbol. To illustrate this, we can take two poetesses, both spinsters, recluses, and religious—Emily Dickinson and Christina Georgina Rossetti. Roughly speaking, Christina Rossetti writes with her intuition, Emily Dickinson with her brain.

For example, Christina Rossetti:

> My heart is like a rainbow shell
>   That paddles in a halcyon sea . . . &c.

but Emily Dickinson:

> On a columnar self
> How ample to rely;
> In tumult or extremity
> How good the certainty
> That lever cannot pry,

> And wedge cannot divide
> Conviction, that granitic base,
> Though none be on our side.

[It must be admitted, of course, that the *music* of Christina Rossetti's verse also contributes to the more sensuous impression.]

But Emily Dickinson's metaphors are not always so coldly cerebral; sometimes they are concrete, give a direct physical impression:

> piles of solid moan,
> And chips of blank in boyish eyes. . . .

I suspect again that in both these mystically minded women their fondness for using jewellery and clothes stuffs as images represents a repressed desire for the actual things.

In Crashaw similarly we have a metaphysical poet who writes from mystical emotion, using his brain, but whose brain or soul throws up images which are often very sensuous:

> The dew no more will weep
> The primrose's pale cheek to deck:
> The dew no more will sleep
> Nuzzel'd in the lily's neck. . . .

If we look back to the Greek and Latin poets who still have such a large, if indirect, influence on our writing, we find that most of these poets used images for the sake of clarity, though the Alexandrians used them for obscurity's sake and many Latin poets for padding. The embroidered 'Latin' simile has often been imitated in English; witness Dryden's 'Annus Mirabilis':

> All hands employ'd, the royal work grows warm:
>   Like labouring bees on a long summer's day,
> Some sound the trumpet for the rest to swarm,
>   And some on bells of tasted lilies play.

But other poets have used the Graeco-Latin simile more functionally, in order, that is, to make sharper the scenes which they are describing. Witness Dante:

> E come i gru van cantando lor lai,
>   facendo in aer di sè lunga riga;
>   così vid' io venir, traendo guai,
> ombre portate dalla detta briga.

'And as the cranes go chanting their lays, making a long streak of themselves in the air: so I saw the shadows come, uttering wails, borne by that strife of winds. . . .'

Metaphor is more concentrated than simile, but more dangerous to poetic law and order. The Greeks, especially Aeschylus and Pindar, were often very daring with metaphor, anticipating many modern experiments. In Aeschylus' choruses the images are often integral to the meaning and suppose their context in such a way that we do not stop to think, 'This is an algebraic symbol for that', but react at once emotionally to the whole. Witness the following portion of a chorus from the 'Agamemnon':

> But the money-changer War, changer of bodies,
> Holding his balance in the battle
> Home from Troy refined by fire
> Sends back to friends the dust
> That is heavy with tears, stowing
> A man's worth of ashes
> In an easily handled jar.

with Headlam's note:

'The God of War is like a money-changer who gives gold for bulkier metal; but his dealing is in flesh and blood; he has his scales like the money-changer, but they are the scales of battle; he receives a human body, a man's bulk, and what he gives back for it in exchange is like the merchant's gold-dust (ψῆγμα), fined in the fire (πυρωθέν), and *heavy*, for it causes heaviness; and packed in vessels which are εὔθετοι, a word covering two senses—"handy", *habiles*, and "decently disposed", *bene compositi*, applied to a corpse. . . .' [This play upon analogies, indeed, approaches the pun. Compare to-day Day Lewis:

> as ocean-flyer caught
> To the last drop of *spirit* driving on [italics mine].

Such concentrated and organic imagery, in which the algebra is correct but the immediate effect physical, is not often met with even in Shakespeare, who often obscures his drift through Alexandrian elaboration or Pindaric confusion, thereby probably having a bad influence on subsequent poets. After Shakespeare came Milton, on the one hand, and the poetry of conceits on the other. Though we should notice that Milton, besides his usual classic similes, not only uses conceits such as

> the blabbing Eastern scout,
> The nice morn on the Indian steep,

but uses, like Crashaw, daring transpositions of images which, while looking back to Shakespeare, look forward to the Symbolists, e.g. of music

> At every fall smoothing the Raven downe
> Of darkness till it smil'd. . . .

Such transposition is familiar to us in certain clichés—we say that a singer *weaves* his notes—but modern poets have used it with exceptional freedom and Joyce has used it often in his prose. Compare E. E. Cummings in 'The Enormous Room', where he speaks of hearing a tune whistled outside a window —'a smooth whistle, cool like a peeled willow-branch'. This is apt (*a*) because such a branch is long and taperingly thin and therefore penetrating, (*b*) a peeled branch being white and fresh, suggests the freshness of the sound, (*c*) willows suggest water and so the fluid quality of this overheard music.

The seventeenth century, on the whole, as compared with the Elizabethans tended to abandon that emotional or sensuous type of image which in the Elizabethans is so often evocative but at the same time blurred. The images of the Caroline poets are sharp and precise. Marvell in his 'Coy Mistress' is extremely suggestive, but by a quick succession of individually sharp images rather than by an intuitive fusion of dissimilars:

> Let us roll all our strength and all
> Our sweetness up into one ball,
> And tear our pleasures with rough strife
> Through the iron gates of life. . . .

Dryden and Pope contented themselves with the more conventional classic metaphors and similes, for clarity's sake dropping both the subtle algebra of the metaphysicals and the word-auras of Shakespeare. But Dr. Johnson in turning his back on the Metaphysical Poets also looks forward to the Romantic Revival: 'Their attempts were always analytick; they broke every image into fragments: and could no more represent, by their slender conceits and laboured particularities, the prospects of nature, or the scenes of life, than he who dissects a sunbeam with a prism can exhibit the *wide effulgence* of a summer morn [italics mine].' The poet's object, this passage at least implies, is to give a general impression roughly appropriate to his subject-matter rather than any clean-cut formula. And we must agree that, as far as the representation of sense objects is concerned, it is impossible ever to render accurately in words the scent of a carnation. But having admitted this to be impossible we still do not know whether it is better to generalize and aim at a wide effulgence or to attempt an 'analytick' approach like that of the Metaphysicals. When we examine representatives of the opposing schools, we see that their use of imagery is adapted to their subject-matter. When Donne saw a sunset he saw something different from what Shelley saw.

The poets of the Romantic Revival use language in their peculiar way because they have a peculiar attitude to life or to the world. 'Nature' is here predominant rather than humanity, and, according as the poet is more interested in natural *objects* or in nature as an impulse, he uses sensuous images intended to convey the appearance or texture of the objects or more fantastic but emotionally exciting images intended to express his sympathy with the nature *behind* the phenomena. Contrast Keats:

> Are not our lowing heifers sleeker than
> Night-swollen mushrooms?

with Shelley:

> the leaves dead
> Are driven, like ghosts from an enchanter fleeing.

The Victorian poets, though less preoccupied with 'Nature', continued to use the Romantic type of image, neither reverting to the cerebral type which was suspect as unpoetic ('Wit' had gone out of poetry) nor working forward to the subtler overtones of the Symbolists (all these distinctions are of course oversimplified; the Symbolists at moments approximate to the Metaphysicals and the wheel comes full circle). Tennyson, the most concrete of the Victorians, had an excellent eye and like Keats uses images to convey the look of objects—a distant waterfall is 'like a downward smoke'. Sometimes he goes further and approaches wit:

> thousand wreaths of dangling water smoke
> That like a broken purpose waste in air. . . .

For the fusion of wit and intuition at this period we have to look across the Channel to Baudelaire. It is worth noting here that Baudelaire's poems are short. In a short poem one image or set of images can more easily be structural, whereas in the longer poems of Tennyson they tend to be episodic; and so one hears of Tennyson's 'vignettes'. Baudelaire is especially fond of images from the seasons which support both the mood and thought of the whole poem. Sometimes like the Romantic Revival poets he uses an easy allegory:

> Vois se pencher les défuntes Années,
> Sur les balcons du ciel, en robes surannées;
> Surgir du fond des eaux le Regret souriant;

Le Soleil moribond s'endormir sous une arche,
Et, comme un long linceul traînant à l'Orient,
Entends, ma chère, entends la douce Nuit qui marche.

Or again:

Quand vers toi mes désirs partent en caravane,
Tes yeux sont la citerne où boivent mes ennuis—

a metaphor with many classical precedents, its novelty
lying solely in the word *ennuis*.

Baudelaire's great quality is concentration, shown
often in the comparison of physical to spiritual and
vice versa:

Et le ver rongera ta peau comme un remords

or

dormir dans l'oubli comme un requin dans l'onde.

But he is not a difficult poet; some of his most
memorable lines are as simple as those of Wordsworth
or Pope:

J'ai peur du sommeil comme on a peur d'un grand trou.

In Baudelaire there is a fine balance between wit
and intuition, statement and suggestion. The Symbolists, his successors, throwing out both rhetoric
and brute reality:

Le sens trop précis rature
Ta vague littérature—

devoted themselves to suggestion. Logical analogies
went out and sensed affinities came in, supported by
music:

Les sanglots longs
Des violons
De l'automne...

Images and properties became fused, as in Rimbaud. Free from the supervision of logic and governed by private associations, poetry became very obscure, as the poets admitted with pride:

'Nommer un objet, c'est supprimer les trois quarts de la jouissance du poème qui est faite du bonheur de dessiner peu à peu; le suggérer, voilà le rêve. C'est le parfait usage de ce mystère qui constitue le symbole.'

The merging of image into property in such poems maintains their status as dreams. Thus Mallarmé's faun says:

> Mon doute, amas de nuit ancienne, s'achève
> En maint rameau subtil . . .

and one is not sure—and one is not meant to be sure —whether he is talking about a metaphorical forest of doubt or about the real wood in which he has been sleeping.

The possibilities of this way of writing are well shown by Mallarmé's sonnet on the Swan, which begins

> Le vierge, le vivace et le bel aujourd'hui
> Va-t-il nous déchirer avec un coup d'aile ivre
> Ce lac dur oublié que hante sous le givre
> Le transparent glacier des vols qui n'ont pas fui!

On which M. Charles Mauron comments:

'The sonnet begins with a great beating of wings, or rather with a hope of flight. It is a fine, blue, frosty winter's morning, with a feeling in the air of excitement and impatience. . . . The lines express a hope of thaw and deliverance. But for the time being the Swan is a prisoner, and the transparent ice, under a thin layer of hoar-frost, reflects the feathers of the bird, "the flights unflown" (a somewhat ghostly reflection, whence the word "haunts"). The two last lines of the quatrain . . . paint with impressionist precision the glassy, dull light of the reflection under the hoar-frost, and the spectral and unreal tonality is reinforced by the use of the abstract "flights" for wings . . . and by the negative of "which have not flown".'

Such a method obviously is magnificent for transmitting an atmosphere, but the atmosphere will tend to be too rarefied. Those who practise imagery in the Symbolist manner would do well occasionally to notice how images are used in ordinary speech, i.e. to drive home a meaning, to make a point, to *outline* a picture (for an outline is distinct from a suggestion). Such images, paradoxically, are often far less *precise* than those of the Symbolists, but they are much more palpable; witness popular analogies for people's faces —'face like a coffin . . . like a muffin . . . like a fish, &c.' Popular images harden into clichés and so lose vividness, no longer call up a picture. But the popular imagination, as shown, for example, in the American wisecrack, is something with which the poet should stay in communion. Poetry can become too niggling. Synge was right when he said 'in countries where the imagination of the people, and the language they use, is rich and living, it is possible for a writer to be rich and copious in his words, and at the same time to give the reality, which is the root of all poetry, in a comprehensive and natural form', but he was wrong in implying that such language is nowadays found only among peasants. Witness the English music-halls or the newspaper articles of many of the sporting journalists, the slang talk of New York or the stories of Ring W. Lardner. A cockney matron at my preparatory school used to say of a boy with prominent teeth, 'There's Master T—— hanging out his teeth to dry', and I have heard a Birmingham gardener say, 'They won't get me for the next war unless they fight with pig's bladders'. This spontaneous colouring of speech is something that the modern poet should emulate. (Compare Chapter X.)

ii

Modernist poetry, as introduced to England by Eliot, inherited its use of imagery both from recent French poets and, among English poets, from the late Elizabethans and the Metaphysicals. Laforgue, together with Donne, contributed to the return of wit. The obscurity of Eliot is not always due to vagueness of suggestion, to a private aura, but is often due to an ellipse; the images themselves are precise but the links between one image and the next are omitted (as is sometimes the case in Pindar).

A *private* poet does not make many concessions to his public. If I write: 'It was as pleasant to me as the 17th of October' the public will not take the point unless I explain that on the 17th of October I received a legacy, but to insert such an explanation will make the comparison cumbrous, like a joke that has to be explained. 'It was as noisy as the 12th of July' would be universally comprehensible in Ulster but not in England. 'It was as new as the 1st of January' would be intelligible anywhere. The images of most poets are like the second type; they require in their readers a certain experience or knowledge which may be expected to be within the reach of a fairly large minority.

The poetry of Eliot and Pound is especially difficult because they use other writers' images *lifted out of their context*. But Eliot is more defensibly difficult when aiming at concentration or wit-effects. In his early poems the images are often properly wit-images:

> When the evening is spread out against the sky
> Like a patient etherized upon a table.

or

> Streets that follow like a tedious argument
> Of insidious intent
> To lead you to an overwhelming question. . . .

and then there will be a switch-over to a sensuous image:

> The yellow fog that rubs its back upon the window panes.

And for Aeschylean concentration witness:

> A current under sea
> Picked his bones in whispers.

And sometimes he approaches surrealism, but there is still an element of wit present as corrective:

> Midnight shakes the memory
> As a madman shakes a dead geranium.

Of the younger poets some have gone on into surrealism, where the difficulty is not due to an ellipse of sense, for the sense was never there (or rather the sense is only half-baked and has never 'found its nature'—the elements have not become bread). Witness Dylan Thomas, even at his more lucid:

Dawn breaks behind the eyes;
From poles of skull and toe the windy blood
Slides like a sea;
Nor fenced, nor staked, the gushers of the sky
Spout to the rod
Divining in a smile the oil of tears.

At first sight this looks as if it might be metaphysical writing, the disguise of a logical idea, but I think on the contrary that it is the almost automatic collocation of a number of emotional (primarily sexual) symbols, thrown up as a drunk man throws up phrases. (But Dylan Thomas is not a typical surrealist in that he obviously allows a technical interest—the sound of the lines—to condition what he writes, whereas the surrealists disown all conscious artistry.) But the general principle of surrealism I shall criticize later.

William Empson, on the other hand, has gone on from Eliot's wit into a purely cerebral jigsaw writing. The meaning is disguised in an unfamiliar algebra (borrowed largely from the sciences), but the meaning is definitely there. I myself find this extreme of writing arid and therefore unpleasant, but it is preferable to surrealism because at least it is not sloppy.

The younger poets whom I most admire, Auden and Spender, write differently from all these poets— Pound and Eliot, Dylan Thomas, William Empson (who so much differ from each other), because they are more interested in the world of concrete people. Empson is interested in formulas for objects but not in anything he can handle. He studies science from an arm-chair. He is no participant. Auden and Spender are participants; their 'spiritual forms'—to use a conception of Blake's—have hands as well as eyes.

So Auden and Spender, who live in a concrete world, tend to use their images neither as merely algebra nor purely aesthetically for the sake of the image itself. They approach, therefore, the parataxis of the early Chinese poets. They verge sometimes on allegory but, as they are primarily interested in what idealist philosophers used to call the concrete universal, they do not often use particular images merely as counters for generalities.

In Auden the imagery is often dramatic, the meaning being absorbed in the image as an actor is absorbed in his part (or, conversely, as the part, as set down on paper, finds its body in the actor). Auden is a very concrete poet who, consciously or unconsciously (probably consciously because he has read much psychology), often uses a dream technique:

> The horns of the dark squadron
> Converging to attack;
> The sound behind our back
> Of glaciers calving.

In dreams the hierarchies of life break down. Distances in time and place, distinctions between things merely thought of and things perceived, are overruled. If I dream I am in England thinking of Australia, I may suddenly see Australia itself either in diagram form as a map or realistically—the blue gums spurting up beyond my garden. If I dream I am reading a book I may suddenly find I am also living the book. If I dream that I hear a word mentioned—say 'porpoise'—I may suddenly see the por-

poise itself materialize. When I say that Auden uses
a dream technique, I mean for instance that he is very
fond of that figure which Aristotle classes as a species
of metaphor—the particular standing for the general.
As in the dream, if porpoises are mentioned, I do not
think of porpoises in general or of 'porpoiseness', but
may even see a particular porpoise crystallize out of
nothing. Hence Auden's notorious catalogues. His
generalities always crystallize into instances and to
keep them clear-cut he often leaves out the links—
the 'as ifs', the 'for examples'; he does not explain
how the porpoise got into the garden.

But Auden is versatile. He often uses the rhetorical
or classical image as practised by A. E. Housman:

> The flag of morn in conqueror's state
> Enters at the English gate:
> The vanquished eve, as night prevails,
> Bleeds upon the road to Wales.

For Auden admires Housman and Housman's turns.
Housman sometimes overdid his turns as in

> The goal stands up, the keeper
> Stands up to keep the goal—

or his conceits as in

> Fall, winter, fall; for he,
>   Prompt hand and headpiece clever,
>   Has woven a winter robe,
> And made of earth and sea
>   His overcoat for ever,
>   And wears the turning globe.

But such writing, while running the risk of vulgarity, is crisp and alive, and Auden is willing to take

anything alive for his model and lump the vulgarity.
Thus his later poems show the influence of popu-
lar wit as exemplified in Cole Porter's songs or in
American folk-ballads; witness 'Cocaine Lil', one of
Auden's favourite ballads:

> Early in the morning, at half past three,
> They were all lit up like a Christmas tree.

As well as using his dream parataxis and his popular rhetoric, Auden uses the cerebral epigram:

> Touching is shaking hands
> On mortgaged lands—

or the traditional method of allegory:

> That later we, though parted then
> May still recall those evenings when
>   Fear gave his watch no look;
> The lion griefs loped from the shade
> And on our knees their muzzles laid
>   And Death put down his book.

The allegory here is still fairly concrete, once more
reminding us of a dream.

Sometimes his metaphors are mere rhetoric and
do not ring true:

> Noble emotions organized and massed
> Line the straight flood-lit tracks of memory
> To cheer your image as it passes by. . . .

but it is rarely that Auden's analogies are ill digested,
fail to become concrete. Often, like Eliot, he achieves
the condensed, significant phrase:

> The rigid promise fractured in the garden.

Sometimes he succeeds with a mixed metaphor:

> And all sway forward on the dangerous flood
> Of history, that never sleeps or dies,
>   And, held one moment, burns the hand.

Often a quick comparison is so pregnant that it implies a whole attitude—an attitude to contemporary religion:

>   cathedrals,
> Luxury liners laden with souls,
> Holding to the east their hulls of stone,
> The high thin rare continuous worship
>   Of the self-absorbed.

or to British nationalism, as in his poem on Dover:

>   the lighthouses
> That guard for ever the made privacy of this bay
> Like twin stone dogs opposed on a gentleman's gate.

Spender's images are not so sharp or self contained as Auden's. He tends to fuse metaphor and subject:

> That programme of the antique Satan
> Bristling with guns on the indented page
> With battleship towering from hilly waves. . . .

But he also achieves the pregnant phrase, as of the 'prisoners' who

> lean their solid eyes against the night

or

> The watching of cripples pass
> With limbs shaped like questions

where the comparison does two things at once.

But Spender's most effective use of imagery is when one image pervades and controls a whole poem, as in the poem beginning 'After they have tired of

the brilliance of cities. . . .' This poem is dominated
by the word 'snow' with its associations of hunger,
universality, and clarity:

> it is death stalks through life
> Grinning white through all faces
> Clean and equal like the shine from snow.

> .   .   .   .   .

> And our strength is now the strength of our bones
> Clean and equal like the shine from snow. . . .

> .   .   .   .   .

> We have come at last to a country
> Where light equal, like the shine from snow, strikes all
>   faces. . . .

> .   .   .   .   .

> But through torn-down portions of old fabric let their eyes
> Watch the admiring dawn explode like a shell
> Around us, dazing us with its light like snow.

Spender in his use of imagery has been influenced
by Hölderlin and Rilke—witness his own, very
Spenderesque, translation of Rilke's 'Hermes, Or-
pheus, Eurydice'. Compare also the bold fusion of
images in Lorca:

> Por las gradas sube Ignacio
> con toda su muerte a cuestas.

In the poem which contains these lines, 'The Lament
for the Death of a Bullfighter', Lorca plays on whole
sets of images, appropriate to his general theme but
transposed in an unexpected way which is perhaps
only a further development of Virgil's well-known
transposition of epithets. Thus the bullfighter's
blood is spoken of as 'stumbling on its thousand
little hoofs'—*tropezando con miles de pezuñas*; every-

thing, from the moon to human life, is thought of in terms of bulls and bullrings; the images spill over and run in blended streams.

I have been discussing here the ways in which images can be used rather than the spheres from which they are taken, for this latter belongs still more properly to the study of subject-matter. I have already maintained that images approximate to properties; from this it follows that images frequently have more in common with their theme than is given by a mere analogy or mathematical parallel. Thus while a poet like Day Lewis, whose theme is the modern industrial world, its economics and its politics, takes his images especially from such things as pylons, power-houses, spies, frontiers, aeroplanes, steam-engines, a poet like Spender, whose approach to the same world, and therefore that world itself, are more mystical, is still very free with the stock mystical symbols—roses, crystal, snow, stars, gold. And a poet like Charles Madge, who is obsessed by curious coincidences, uses images from astrology.

I find that I use images myself (*a*) to clarify a picture, (*b*) to express an idea with more concentration and more shock to the reader than it would have if stated baldly or explicitly. I allow myself the use of many different types of image, for example, the sensuous type:

> The murderous grin of toothy flowers

or (of the sea):

> With Thor's thunder or taking his ease akimbo
> Lumbering torso, but finger-tips a marvel
> Of surgeon's accuracy.

though here the sensuous effect is largely due to onomatopoeic writing.

I also use the cerebral image:

> The minnow-twistings of the latinist who alone
> Nibbles and darts through the shallows of the lexicon.

and the blend of cerebral and sensuous as (of aeroplanes):

> When these tiny flies like nibs will calmly draw our death
> A dipping gradient on the graph of Europe.

This last is almost a metaphysical image, but the picture of the moving aeroplanes is intended to persist.

Sometimes, more fantastically, I take several images and ring the changes on them. Thus in a philosophical poem, 'Homage to Clichés', I think of the brute Other, the fate which we cannot influence: (*a*) as an Egyptian Rameses, (*b*) as a tenor bell (which we cannot peal but can only play chimes upon), (*c*) as a black panther (black because unknown and because the black panther is popularly said to be untamable). The movement of each of these three will be the movement of Fate:

> The ringers are taking off their coats, the panther crouches,
> The granite sceptre is very slightly inclining. . . .

The present trend, however, is to reduce images in proportion to properties. This is because, as I have said, poets are now more interested in subject, and that a subject from the concrete objective world. The few poets to-day who, like Laura Riding, Robert Graves, and Norman Cameron, philosophize in their poetry, *have* to use images because bare philosophy belongs to science rather than to poetry. Witness Norman Cameron's excellent poem on the principle of Love:

> He bloomed in our bodies to the finger-tips
> And rose like barley-sugar round the lips.

But most of the other poets 'philosophize', if they do philosophize, more in the manner of Wordsworth. For Wordsworth the objective world of nature is an embodiment, not a concealment, of something like the Platonic Forms. He does not therefore require many images because his properties carry their own message.

VII

RHYTHM AND RHYME

WE are always hearing that modern poets do not write for the ear. As I very much like the sound of much modern poetry, and as I nearly always write for the ear myself, I shall now try to discuss modern poetry as music. But it must be remembered that rhythm in poetry is in one respect essentially different from rhythm in music, in that poetry always carries a meaning and this meaning has inevitable repercussions on the rhythm.

Mr. G. M. Young in an attack on modern versification stated that it ignores 'the fundamental distinction between stated and emergent rhythm' (though he would allow, inconsistently, the hybrid verse used by Sacheverell Sitwell in 'Canons of Giant Art'). Mr. Young says that English poetry has always relied upon stated rhythm and that it is stated rhythm which distinguishes it from prose. The rhythmical pattern, unlike that of prose, must be recognizable. Now I have already stated that I do not recognize any great gulf between poetry and prose. Roughly speaking, the poet wants his *words* to be listened to or looked at more than the prose-writer does. But some prose-writers want their words looked at more than some poets do. However, if it is granted that the poet wants his words looked at or listened to, he will naturally arrange them towards this end. And he will find that if he arranges them in certain repetitive patterns this repetition will hold the reader's attention and unify the writing. For example, if a word A is expecting its rhyme a four lines on, the reader will tend to remember A at least till he gets to a; whereas in reading prose one tends rather to forget the parts in hustling on towards the end—which is the total meaning.

Metre, verse-pattern, and rhyme are therefore conveniences for the poet, but they are not laws of nature. If he can do without them, he is entitled to. I think myself that poetry which has very little rhythm tends to be boring, but hold that, once there is a pattern, the pattern is often more effective the more it is varied. Whether these variations are re-cognized as variations *of a pattern* will depend upon the reader and, while I think that a poet should make allowances for his readers, I should never ask him to moderate his pace to suit the slowest members of his audience. As Gerard Manley Hopkins said, 'in every-thing the more remote the ratio of the parts to one another or the whole the greater the unity if felt at all'. But who is to decide if it is felt at all—Mr. G. M. Young or the poet himself? Or should we not again posit an ideal normal reader, sympathetic to the poet but not a member of his clique, with a natural liking for poetry, of fair education, but with-out academic bias?

To take the extreme case of 'free verse'—Mr. Young suggests that it is only distinguished from prose by its typographical arrangement on the page. But such an arrangement deploys the lines and phrases in such a way that we at least get a better view of them than if they were printed as prose. The words are more *poised* than in prose; they are not only, like the words in typical prose, contributory to the total effect, but are to be attended to, in passing, for their own sake. In typical prose each sentence forgets the sentence preceding. The contrast between verse and prose is like the contrast between rugby football and games like netball. The mere arranging of verse in lines serves the same purpose as the off-side rule in rugger and the rule against forward passes; instead of the meaning being passed vertically down the field as it is in prose, each line in verse when it comes to an end passes back to the beginning of the next (and I am not only thinking of typography). This method, as in rugger, gives a sweeping movement, an impression of controlled speed and power—an impression which is enhanced when the verse is on a recognizable rhythmical pattern.

I would admit then the legitimacy of even the baldest free verse where the rhythms are not variants on one or several dominant rhythms but come out haphazard like the names in a telephone directory. I can see that the phrases in such verse can be more poised and therefore more effective and memorable than if merged in the hurry-scurry of prose. Witness D. H. Lawrence on a baby tortoise (though much free verse has far less obvious rhythm than this example which, if repeated strophically, could become an easily recognizable pattern):

> Moving, and being himself,
> Slow, and unquestioned,

And inordinately there, O stoic!
Wandering in the slow triumph of his own existence,
Ringing the soundless bell of his presence in chaos,
And biting the frail grass arrogantly,
Decidedly arrogantly.

I would also admit that some valuable poetry which
is in the form of free verse could not have come to
birth either in regular verse or in prose—witness
especially Whitman. But in general I myself prefer
the more regular kinds of verse because I think that
if you are going to poise your phrases at all they
will usually need more poise than can be given them
by the mere arranging of them in lines. Few poets
have the *élan* of Whitman or Lawrence and most
free verse, consequently, is thin and not memorable.
Further, the poet's *matter* tends in this form to appear insufficiently digested or distilled; a technical
problem often helps a poet to get his own meaning
clear to himself.

But granting that a rhythmical basis, known or
sensed, is an asset to a poem, I think that many
poems (especially those which come from more
subtle or sophisticated subjects or moods) are the
better for rhythmical variations, (*a*) because rhythmical variations can often be significant of variations
in content, (*b*) because variety is delightful for its
own sake. Mr. Young, intending a *reductio ad absur-
dum* of modern metric, brings up 'Johnson's friend,
who thought that if a line had ten syllables it was
verse':

Put your knife and your fork across your plate.

Now it is obvious that the rhythm of this line is not

a rhythm fit to be repeated through all or most of the lines of a poem whose basis is taken to be the regular blank verse basis ∪ – ∪ – ∪ – ∪ – ∪ –. But it is not obvious that such a line is unfit to enter such a poem at all. – ∪ – ∪ ∪ – ∪ – ∪ – is a recognizable variation on the blank verse line and as such may have its own emotional significance. For example, in a poem of melodrama describing an impending murder:

> The dark is falling and the hour is late:
> *Put your knife and your fork across your plate.*

Here the change from the neat traditional rhythm of the first line to the halting rhythm of the second, which throws an additional stress on 'knife' and 'fork', would to my ear have a sinister effect entirely in keeping with the subject. Broken rhythms have their uses, as have merely flat or pedestrian lines, or hiatus, which in itself is normally unpleasant; thus 'the empty air' merely as sound is much emptier than 'the vacant air'.

In English poetry we have many magnificent examples of strict metrical regularity—the liquid regularity of Chaucer and Spenser, the metal regularity of the heroic couplet. But we have as many specimens of less regular verse which while not attaining the effects of the former, attains other effects which are out of the former's reach. Apart from our earlier verse—*Piers Plowman* or Skelton—most of the writers of blank verse, from Shakespeare to Swinburne, have introduced variations—'counterpointing'—which we accept because we are aware of the basic rhythm on which they are variations. Witness

Of Mán's Fírst Disobédience and the Frúit

where, apart from the very strong counterpointing of the second foot, the whole line appears to have only four stresses instead of five. Milton gives us still subtler depatternings in the choruses of *Samson Agonistes*. Shakespeare, in his later dramatic verse, often uses more naturalistic variations:

> You do look, my son, in a moved sort
> As if you were dismayed.

I choose these lines deliberately because they are suspect; they may be spurious lines or they may be a corruption, but they are good lines with a rhythm which is emotionally most apt. (In fact, that un-intended rhythms may sometimes be more effective than those intended can be seen by a re-reading of Chaucer as the Elizabethans read him, in a four-stress 'rough-riding' measure. Much is lost but something is gained.)

But as an example of a poem whose rhythmical variations are frequent, subtle, and certainly in-tended, I will take the first four verses of the famous lyric by Nashe:

> I. 1. Adieu, farewell earth's bliss!
>   2. This world uncertain is:
>   3. Fond are life's lustful joys,
>   4. Death proves them all but toys.
>   5. None from his darts can fly;
>   6. I am sick, I must die—
>   Lord, have mercy on us.
>
> II. 1. Rich men, trust not in wealth,
>   2. Gold cannot buy you health;
>   3. Physic himself must fade;
>   4. All things to end are made;

      5. The plague full swift goes by;
      6. I am sick, I must die—
         Lord, have mercy on us.

III. 1. Beauty is but a flower
      2. Which wrinkles will devour;
      3. Brightness falls from the air;
      4. Queens have died young and fair;
      5. Dust hath closed Helen's eye;
      6. I am sick, I must die—
         Lord, have mercy on us!

IV. 1. Strength stoops unto the grave,
      2. Worms feed on Hector brave;
      3. Swords may not fight with fate;
      4. Earth still holds ope her gate;
      5. *Come, come!* the bells do cry;
      6. I am sick, I must die—
         Lord, have mercy on us.

Of these four verses, with the exception of the refrain, I offer the following analysis, using four signs instead of the usual two.

  = represents a heavily stressed syllable.
  — represents a stressed syllable which is not so heavy.
  · represents an unstressed syllable.
  : represents an unstressed syllable which carries a little more weight.

[This notation is of course only very roughly approximate. The cymograph has proved how great are the merely quantitative variations of spoken syllables; in poetry we must remember further that the syllables are more than mere counters; the meaning of the word also affects its stress so that 'God', in spite of mere sound-value, is a more telling monosyllable than 'goad'.]

I. 1. · = : = — =
    2. = — · = · —
    3. = · = = · =
    4. = — · = · =
    5. = · — = · =
    6. — · = — · =

II. 1. = : = — · =
    2. = · : = · =
    3. = · · = · =
    4. = — · = · =
    5. · = : = · =
    6. — · = — : =

III. 1. = · : — · =   [or = · — : · = , an equivo-
                        cation of rhythm itself signi-
                        ficant.]
     2. · = · — · =
     3. = · = : · =
     4. = · = = · =
     5. = · = = · =
     6. — · = — · =

IV. 1. = = : · · =
    2. = = · = · =
    3. = : · = · =   [or = · : = · =]
    4. = : = = · =   [or = = : = · =]
    5. = = · = · =
    6. — · = — · =

It is misleading to apply to this poem terms taken from quantitative prosody. The first line of the first verse, if found elsewhere, might easily be labelled iambic:

> Adieú, farewéll earth's blíss (three stresses)

but it is obvious, as we read on, that the lines are written on a four-stress basis, but so varying that we cannot pin them down to a cretic (– ◡ –) or to any other one-foot system. The lines, indeed, end fairly regularly with something like a cretic, but the first three syllables of the lines are beautifully varied with great emotional effect; witness the opening of the fourth verse, where the heavy stresses come together:

> Strength stoops unto the grave,
> Worms feed on Hector brave. . . .

Many modern poets dislike strait-jacketed verse. They would like to attain to the musical subtlety of Nashe, but they often have another, more naturalistic, reason for changes of rhythm in that they wish to keep closer to the rhythms of spoken conversation. In much English verse the irregularities can be explained, in Hopkins's term, as counterpointing. Hopkins also introduced the term 'sprung rhythm' to describe another kind of irregular rhythm which, according to him, was different in kind from counterpointing.

To my ear this difference is only a difference in degree. English verse is not quantitative and therefore ordinary blank verse lines, whatever their degree of counterpointing, do not merely consist of five long syllables plus five shorts or, if preferred, of five stressed plus five unstressed. The longs and the shorts all differ between themselves; there are all sorts of half-stresses, three-quarter stresses, distributed stresses. Thus in Milton's line

> Of Mán's Fírst Disobédience and the Frúit

I cannot find a fifth syllable worthy to be matched against those which I have marked.[1]

---

[1] The word 'and' here admittedly can be stressed, but it will not be such a heavy stress..

Now in a sentence of ordinary conversation we tend to stress only a few syllables in proportion to quite a large number of unstressed—'Jóhn was going to get the cár out when he tumbled over the vácuum cleaner.' But sometimes conversation groups the stresses together—'Jóhn's dámned dóg bít my lég.' English verse on the contrary generally steers a middle course, tending to apportion the stresses in the ratio of one to two or one to three syllables. Hopkins wanted to introduce the licence of conversation into verse. His eye was on the Old English models and he thought that by limiting the *number* of stresses but apportioning them where he liked in the line, he would be able to achieve (*a*) the naturalistic richness of conversation, but not dissipated, as it is in conversation, by the lack of a formal basis, and (*b*) variety of rhythm for variety's sake.

Such a licence, besides being practised in popular ballads and nursery rhymes, had already been claimed as the poet's right by Coleridge in his preface to 'Christabel':

'I have only to add that the metre of "Christabel" is not, properly speaking, irregular, though it may seem so from its being founded on a new principle: namely, that of counting in each line the accents, not the syllables. Though the latter may vary from seven to twelve, yet in each line the accents will be found to be only four. Nevertheless, this occasional variation in the number of syllables is not introduced wantonly, or for the mere ends of convenience, but in correspondence with some transition in the nature of the imagery or the passion.'

Hopkins and Coleridge were both entitled to

demand this licence, but were both mistaken in thinking they could sanction it merely by the counting of
stressed syllables, as is shown in Hopkins's own practice where the counting is often a fraud. Witness
(with Hopkins's own stress-marks):

Christ minds; Christ's interest, what to avow or mend
> There, eýes them, heart wánts, care haúnts, foot follows
> kínd,
Their ránsom, théir rescue, ánd first, fást, last friénd.

These are strong and effective lines, but Hopkins's
notation makes them vicious. Merely through stick-
ing to his fetish of five stresses per line, he (*a*) goes
miles away from his admired rhythms of ordinary
speech, and (*b*) (which matters much more) slurs over,
as unstressed, words—'heart', 'care', 'rescue', 'first',
'last'—which, both for their sound-value and their
meaning, *ought not* to be slurred over.

I do not myself think that a stress more or less in
a line matters much more than an unstressed syllable more or less attached to a stress. These differences are only of degree, and success or failure
depends on whether the total pattern is broken. The
Alexandrine, after all, has always been regarded as
a legitimate variation in blank verse. But valuable
syllables ought not, where possible, to be slurred
over. 'Pussy-cat, Pussy-cat, where have you been?'
is a good line rhythmically, but I should not like to
write, 'Pólar Bear, Pólar Bear, where have you been?'
For (*a*) in ordinary speech we say 'Pólar Beár' and
(*b*) 'bear' is here a more important syllable than
'-cat' both for sound-value and meaning. (I would
admit, of course, that there are cases where a fine

effect is gained by making a strong syllable fight against its position in the line.)

Hopkins's influence on younger poets to-day has often been unfortunate. A close imitation of his manner is dangerous because both his rhythms and his syntax were peculiarly appropriate to his own un-usual circumstances and his own tortured but vital personality:

> Thou mastering me
> God! giver of breath and bread;
> World's strand, sway of the sea;
> Lord of living and dead . . .

is religious poetry even in its rhythms.

Poets like Eliot made a more genuine compromise with ordinary speech rhythms, writing verse portions of which, like some verse in drama, was itself on the conversational plane. I could not attempt a metrical analysis of 'The Waste Land' or 'Gerontion', but would deny that in such poems the conversational element submerged the music of the poem as a whole. Often in Eliot the traditional blank-verse line is an implicit basis for his versification, but he allows him-self to break away from it quickly just as he allows himself to switch quickly from one kind of diction or one set of images or one picture to another. Eliot's verse, like a film, relies in every respect very much on its 'cutting'.

The poets of *New Signatures* have reacted, rhyth-mically as in other ways, towards homogeneity. Their verse is usually identifiable as verse throughout. They do not change key so often as Eliot or Pound. Their rhythmical variations are not so much in the cause of dramatic naturalism, but in order to signify some *personal* change of tone[1] or for the negative reason that they are afraid of too pat and regular a form as being liable to blunt the reader's sensibility or lull him to slumber. Auden, however, and others are moving back towards fairly regular stanza forms in their lyrics, recognizing that tricks such as those of Nashe or Housman give a poet a good deal of play within the form itself. In their longer poems, however, which are contemplative or didactic, they tend to keep the form loose as being more adaptable to the thought.

Apart from the question of significant variation, of adaptability to content, some forms in English have been overworked and, if used at all, must be used with a certain novelty because otherwise they will be too reminiscent of too familiar models. This is especially so with blank verse. Traditional blank verse is, for the young poet, like a large leather arm-chair in a club; once he gets into it, there he is for the afternoon. Witness the depressing specimens of Shakespearian and Wordsworthian blank verse (though written partly with the tongue in the cheek) in 'The Ascent of F6'. The poet to-day, I suggest, should use blank verse with freedom, varying the length of the lines and the grouping of the stresses; and he must also avoid (what he is still more liable to suffer in the sonnet) falling into obsolete turns of

---

[1] For a significant change of rhythm compare Donne:
    Let mee prepare towards her, and let mee call
    This houre her Vigill, and her Eve, since this
    Both the yeares, and the dayes deep midnight is.

phrase which blank verse automatically will suggest
to him.

Here is an example of verse loosened in the right
way from an early poem by Auden:

> But happy now, though no nearer each other,
> We see the farms lighted all along the valley;
> Down at the mill-shed the hammering stops
> And men go home.
>
> Noises at dawn will bring
> Freedom for some, but not this peace
> No bird can contradict; passing but is sufficient now
> For something fulfilled this hour, loved or endured.

A great deal is lost, purely in rhythm, if we transpose
this into a more regular metre:

> But happy now, although no nearer others,
> We see the farms lit up along the valley;
> Below—the hammering at the mill-shed stops
> And men go home.
> The sounds of dawn will bring
> To some their freedom but to none this peace
> No bird can contradict, which passing is enough
> For something felt this hour, endured or loved.

Spender habitually resolves his rhythms, attaining
thereby the poise of some one balancing on an edge
rather than the security of a man on the ground or on
a pedestal:

> They think how one life hums, revolves and toils,
> One cog in a golden and singing hive:
> Like spark from fire, its task happily achieved,
> It falls away quietly.

The variations here are slight, but if we strait-jacket
the verse we see what an asset they were:

> They think how one life hums, revolves and toils,
> A single cog in a golden, singing hive;
> Like spark from fire, its happy task achieved,
> It quietly falls away [or It falls away in quiet].

In my own practice I find that a poem of the blank-
verse kind, unless short, usually requires pedestrian
lines as foils to the others; every line should not
be equally heightened. And blank verse should be
strong rather than pretty. For this reason syllables
naturally weighted should be given their weight instead of the weight being shared out over the line.

> The Polar Bear prowled on the ice

is a better line than

> The Polar Bear was prowling on the ice.

What classical metrical theorists would call the 'synco-
pation' of the former line throws a proper stress
on to all the important words, which is dissipated
in the latter line.

Some poets of Georgian upbringing also have
experimented in significant rhythm. Witness that
excellent technician, Edmund Blunden's, 'Report on
Experience':

> I have been young, and now am not too old;
> And I have seen the righteous forsaken,
> His health, his honour and his quality taken.
> This is not what we were formerly told.

But the highly subtle experiments of poets like Blunden and Walter de la Mare are not so open as those

of the younger poets to the charge of irresponsibility; this is because their rhythmical pattern, however subtle, is more clearly *stated*. Much of the younger poets' verse appears rough by comparison because the reader feels he is without clues to the pattern of it.

An important influence on recent verse has been the Anglo-Saxon, one of the first examples being Ezra Pound's poem actually from the Anglo-Saxon, 'The Seafarer':

> Lest man know not
> That he on dry land loveliest liveth,
> List how I, care-wretched, on ice-cold sea
> Weathered the winter, wretched outcast
> Deprived of my kinsmen. . . .

This technique, though often modified, has been copied by many poets—especially the alliteration and the caesura. Witness Eliot in 'Murder in the Cathedral':

> Spring has come in winter. Snow in the branches
> Shall float as sweet as blossoms. Ice along the ditches
> Mirror the sunlight. Love in the orchard
> Send the sap shooting. Mirth matches melancholy.

[The effect of universality attained by the lack of articles does not belong, of course, to a discussion of rhythm.]

Or witness again Day Lewis:

> As one who wanders into old workings
> Dazed by the noonday, desiring coolness,
> Has found retreat barred by fall of rockface;
> Gropes through galleries where granite bruises

> Taut palm and panic patters close at heel;
> Must move forward as time to the moon's nod,
> As mouth to breast in blindness is beckoned.

This Anglo-Saxon versification was at least not stale through recent over-use. Another model who was revived for a little was Skelton, whose metric was copied by both Robert Graves and Auden. Witness Graves:

> He said: 'I cock my mirror above the cage-wires,
>   And through the side window what visions I see!
> The whole world of men and their dismal desires,
>   Fortune tellers, feather ticklers, the crystal sea,
>   Corky angels twanging the tunes of Tennessee,
> Pearly gates, golden streets, a cokernut shy,
> The moral peepshow pandering to the prurient eye.'

Such a model was obviously mainly appropriate to humorous or satirical writing, a field in which Auden at least has picked his models very eclectically but with great success.

After so much energy spent both in breaking away from the tyranny of one set of models and in digging up others which had been forgotten, these younger poets are now reaching a stage where they can write more freely; an arduous technical apprenticeship has brought them to a point where they can let their subject dictate and their technique is able to keep up with it. Thus Auden now often uses conventional verse-forms, but, thanks to his catholic training, their conventionality does not kill their content.

As for rhyme, rhyme also is returning. The case for rhyme is that it is in itself attractive—musical—and makes for memorability (besides setting the poet a healthy technical problem). The case against rhyme is that, being obviously artificial, it suggests insincerity and that it lulls the reader into a pleasant coma. There are many ways in which one may compromise between these two schools of thought. One can use rhyme in a poem, but not continuously or not in the expected places (compare 'Lycidas'). One can use internal rhymes, off-rhymes, bad rhymes, 'pararhymes'; one can rhyme a stressed against an unstressed syllable. Such devices can be used for some onomatopoeic significance (a 'bad' rhyme often having a peculiar emotional effect) or, less positively in order to avoid a total effect which is too pat, smug, commonplace. (I do not suggest that a complete poem of perfect rhymes need be any of these things, but it is a danger of which all poets must be conscious.)

Yeats is a great exponent of the bad rhyme, adopted, no doubt, as part of his programme to make his poetry less 'poetic'. Certain bad rhymes have always been allowed by English convention, for example 'love' and 'prove' or 'happily' and 'tree'. But the poem where such rhymes are the rule rather than the exception is a modern innovation. Witness Yeats:

> A living man is blind and drinks his drop.
> What matter if the ditches are impure?
> What matter if I live it all once more?
> Endure that toil of growing up;
> The ignominy of boyhood; the distress
> Of boyhood changing into man;
> The unfinished man and his pain
> Brought face to face with his own clumsiness.

And Auden has used it a great deal:

> Now in this season when the ice is loosened,
> In scrubbed laboratories research is hastened
> And cameras at the growing wood
> Are pointed; for the long lost good,
> Desire like a police-dog is unfastened.

There are three advantages in this type of rhyme: (1) Such rhymes are still comparatively novel and therefore command attention. (2) They often can be used (see the examples from Yeats above) to give an effect of muted seriousness: (3) While still imposing a helpful limit on the poet and giving the poem an additional structural element, they give the poet a wider and newer range of words to choose from.

Of other favourite modern devices the most notable is the 'pararhyme' invented by Wilfred Owen:

> Our brains ache, in the merciless iced east winds that knive
> us . . .
> Wearied we keep awake because the night is silent . . .
> Lone, drooping flares confuse our memory of the salient .
> Worried by silence, sentries whisper, curious, nervous,
> But nothing happens.

Here the device itself is largely contributory to the total effect of depression and anxiety. Auden has used it largely, and also Graves (the rhymes being more often masculine).

A less serviceable device (also on the whole more appropriate to solemnity than to gaiety) is the rhyming of stressed against unstressed syllables. Graves and Auden have both used this in three-line stanzas, the third rhyme being unstressed. Thus Graves:

O love, be fed with apples while you may
And feel the sun and go in royal array,
A smiling innocent on the heavenly causeway.

And Auden:

Watch any day his nonchalant pauses, see
His dextrous handling of a wrap as he
Steps after into cars, the beggar's envy.

'There is a free one' many say, but err.
He is not that returning conqueror,
Nor ever the poles' circumnavigator.

Unlike Auden or Day Lewis, Spender avoids the formalism of rhyme, which he seems to consider vulgar. Most of his verse is unrhymed, just as most of it is not in regular stanzas. But just as his verse is sometimes in modest stanzas, so it sometimes contains the ghosts of rhymes, as in the following:

Now over these small hills they have built the concrete
That trails black wire:
Pylons, those pillars
Bare like nude, giant girls that have no secret.

But far above and far as sight endures
Like whips of anger
With lightning's danger
There runs the quick perspective of the future.

Here the balance of the end words is still perceptible and therefore pleasurable, but that particular pleasure is lost if one resolves the rhymes much further.

In Chapter X I shall point out that modern poets have come to terms with popular verse and doggerel, Auden here showing the way as usual. Doggerel writers quite often attain good, and special, effects

without having aimed at them. The same can be said
of some professional poets such as Emily Dickinson,
who can rise from what is practically doggerel:

> I walked as wings of body bore,
> The feet I former used
> Unnecessary now to me
> As boots would be to birds

into something which makes doggerel a virtue:

> I clutched at sands—I groped at shapes—
> I touched the tops of films,
> I felt the wilderness roll back
> Along my golden lines.

> The sack cloth hangs upon the nail,
> The frock I used to wear,
> But where my moment of brocade—
> My drop of India?

The sound and shape of this obviously contribute to
the excellent total effect, but this poem may once
again remind us that no formal element in a poem
can properly be divorced from its content. This
must be remembered in my next chapter, on Diction.

As a last word on rhythm and rhyme, and also on
alliteration and texture and sound-value generally, I
would say that my own preference is for poetry which
is musical, but that the characteristics of this music
are not superficial prettiness or smoothness, but (a)
system and (b) significance. When I write poetry
myself, I always consider the sound of each line
conjointly with its adequacy as meaning. I could not
reduce my instincts in this matter to a set of definite
rules. On the whole I avoid difficult mouthfuls of

words or, say, conglomerations of aspirates, but what I positively aim at is something other than mere smoothness. Sometimes I am conscious that a line is roughly onomatopoeic, but I do not think it is possible *deliberately* to suit the sound continuously to the sense. I suspect that here again a poet has to compromise between poetry as representation and poetry as creation, between something recorded and something invented. If one writes a poem about the noise of a waterfall, one may by onomatopoeia make the waterfall 'live again', but only in a sense; but one also *ipso facto* makes something live which is a new noise and not the noise of the waterfall—and which also, of course, is a great deal more than noise.

VIII

DICTION

ARISTOTLE, with his usual facility for separating things which are only λόγῳ χωριστά, speaks of diction very much as if it were a dress to be put on in various pieces. His argument is conditioned by the practice of Greek tragedians who had a whole set of words or forms of words, obsolete in ordinary speech, which were allowed and indeed expected to be used in tragedy. Aristotle accordingly advocates conscious decoration, though, with his usual concern for measure, he insists that such decorations must not be overdone. He says, for example, of Nouns: 'a Noun must be either (1) the ordinary word for the thing, or (2) a strange [i.e. foreign] word, or (3) a metaphor, or (4) an ornamental word, or (5) a coined word, or (6) a word lengthened out, or (7) curtailed, or (8) altered in form.' These last seven types, he holds, are required by poetry as seasoning; compounds are most in place in the dithyramb, 'strange' words in heroic, and metaphors in iambic poetry.

Now obviously a metaphor, as we have seen, can *add* something to a poet's statement or help to convey his meaning with especial economy and concentration. But some of these other decorations tend to dissipate or blunt the meaning. The poetic diction of the Greeks was sanctioned by religion; going to a Greek tragedy was like going to church. Such a sanction is valid because this heightening of diction is correlated with a function which was not yet obsolete. But 'poetic diction' in the modern sense means, at its narrowest, the regular substitution of a more refined (i.e. usually more obsolete) type of word for its vulgar synonym, e.g. 'sire' for 'father'. And nowadays we have no valid sanction for such substitutions. Other things being equal, we may choose between two synonyms by reference to their sound-value, but how few pairs of words are really synonyms. Similarly, the lengthening or curtailment of words—'lovéd' for 'lov'd', 'tawn' (as used by Ezra Pound) for 'tawny'—may be occasionally allowed for prosodic reasons, but should on the whole be avoided as such devices have a quick, but cheap, 'poetic' effect which leaves a bad taste in the mouth.

It was this narrow devotion to an archaic refinement that called forth Wordsworth's merited attack on Poetic Diction, though, like most rebels against a stifling tradition, he very much overstated his case. His fallacies were duly exploded by Coleridge in *Biographia Literaria*. We may add that Wordsworth was inconsistent in not applying his principles to metre as well as to diction; the language of poetry, for him, is not to be distinguished from the language of prose, but metre is a *legitimate* embellishment. Analysis would have proved that any formal trick, whether of language or rhythm, is a *convenience* to the poet. There are no fixed laws of metre any more than there are fixed laws of diction. If Wordsworth denied the latter laws he might well have gone farther and denied the former. This resolution of poetry, this recognition that there are no fixed laws dividing poetry from prose but only conveniences, would have brought him round full circle (as has happened in the evolution of modern poetry) to the recognition that the poet aims at special effects difficult to attain in prose and that therefore he is entitled to adopt any conveniences towards this end, provided that they do not defeat this end by hardening into intractable *sine qua nons* (as had happened with the poetic diction which Wordsworth attacked, or as happened with Latin rhetoric or with the Latin hexameter under the Roman Empire).

Wordsworth's Preface to the *Lyrical Ballads* is, however, very sympathetic to a modern writer. 'Among the qualities . . . principally conducing to form a Poet, is implied nothing differing in kind from other men but only in degree.' As has been seen already, I whole-heartedly agree with this and sympathize with Wordsworth again when he says, 'I have wished to keep the reader in the company of flesh and blood, persuaded that by so doing I shall interest him'. But who is to decide what is the company of flesh and blood? Are the Idiot Boy and Simon Lee more flesh and blood than the glorified heroes of Pindar or even than Belinda in 'The Rape of the Lock'? Just as when Wordsworth speaks of 'the real language of men', who is to decide what is the real language of men? Wordsworth decided that it is the language of real men, i.e. rustics—a piece of self-deception properly exposed by Coleridge.

Agreeing, however, with Wordsworth on the first principle, that the poet differs from other men not in kind but in degree, I draw the natural corollary that there is a similar difference, in degree but not in kind, between the poet's language and ordinary language. This difference in degree is a very important one. For example, ordinary people—whether rustics or not—employ in ordinary conversation much useless repetition and many incoherent anacolutha, which would make very poor reading if taken down verbatim. The poet has to select and concentrate; one step farther and he is changing the word-order, using a specialized syntax, employing all kinds of devices to atone for the lack of the one great asset, which the speakers had and he has not, the tones of the spoken voice. Prose is more distilled than spoken speech; poetry more distilled than prose.

The diction of a poet is very intimately connected with his subject-matter. When the diction has outlived the subject-matter it becomes a burden. New subject-matter therefore needs a new diction. Wordsworthian 'Nature', Godwin's theories, Byron's 'Don Juan', would have been obscured by the diction of the eighteenth century. But it seems to me almost as wrong to say that Pope's diction was false as to say that Georgian architecture or snuff-boxes were false. Both were suited to their period. It is easier to attack the diction of the 'Ancient Mariner', just as it is easier to attack the architecture of Strawberry Hill.

It is often brought against modern poets that their diction is not poetic enough. This may mean one of two things—either that certain of the modern poets' subjects ought not to be treated in poetry at all, or that any subject treated in poetry requires a certain kind of dressing. To take the second point first, while it may often be legitimate to use one of the types of substitute words mentioned above by Aristotle, it is *always* legitimate to use the ordinary word for anything one is writing about. As for the first point, I have already stated that I consider no subject-matter taken from life to be alien to poetry (Wordsworth, generous to a fault to the life of the rustic, disallowed the life of the townee). I am still astonished to meet people who hold that machines or physiology or slums or politics must not be introduced into poetry. Some, less absolute, say that no subject should be treated till the public or some particular public has acquired an emotional relationship to it. Thus a poetess told me that the train was established as a poetic subject, but not the motorcar. I would agree that the poet especially wants to deal with subjects which are of vital interest to his readers, but this reasoning leads to just those subjects against which these objections are usually aimed. How many people to-day have not some emotional relationship to machines or politics? And how many people are not more interested in the problem of evil —in slums or war—than they are in the collecting of bric-à-brac?

While I agree with Wordsworth that the poet ought to keep in touch with flesh and blood, I agree with Aristotle that poetry can often be more effective if its language is heightened. But this heightening must be appropriate. Thus Tennyson in his lyrics uses a language perfectly wedded to a content which is personal and rarefied. But when describing a contemporary scene outside his personal emotions he heightens his language (while seeming to write simply and objectively) according to a formula which does not ring true but reduces the flesh and blood before him to the level of his Knights of the Round Table:

> So sang the gallant glorious chronicle;
> And, I all rapt in this, 'Come out', he said,
> 'To the Abbey: there is Aunt Elizabeth
> And sister Lilia with the rest.' We went
> (I kept the book and had my finger in it)
> Down thro' the park: strange was the sight to me;
> For all the sloping pasture murmur'd, sown
> With happy faces and with holiday.
> There moved the multitude, a thousand heads:
> The patient leaders of their Institute
> Taught them with facts. One rear'd a font of stone
> And drew, from butts of water on the slope,
> The fountain of the moment, playing now
> A twisted snake, and now a rain of pearls,
> Or steep-up spout whereon the gilded ball
> Danced like a wisp: and somewhat lower down
> A man with knobs and wires and vials fired
> A cannon: Echo answered in her sleep
> From hollow fields: and here were telescopes
> For azure views; and there a group of girls
> In circle waited, whom the electric shock
> Dislink'd with shrieks and laughter. . . .

This contemporary conversation-piece seems to me a flat failure. Tennyson quite rightly holds that a fête in a rich man's park is a subject for poetry and rightly attempts (at least I think he is attempting) to describe it realistically. But the piece is castrated to start with through his selection of material; he omits the paper-bag element, the perspiration, the giggles. Secondly, the metre is not limber enough for the subject. Thirdly (which concerns us here), he sets out, as a writer of narrative verse, to write simply:

> I kept the book and had my finger in it—

but cannot resist a few turns to keep it poetic, and the turns and the simplicity do not mix. The mechanical 'amusements' are too laboriously 'written up'. The rather naïve amateur's description:

> A man with knobs and wires and vials [a suspect word] fired
> A cannon

is taken up incongruously by a stock poetic image— 'Echo answered in her sleep . . .'. And I do not like here the grammatical inversion—'strange was the sight to me', or 'I *all rapt* in this' or '*rear'd* a font of stone' or '*whereon* the gilded ball' or '*azure* views'. But perhaps my dislike of the writing here can be referred back to my suspicion of Tennyson's attitude. The piece does not convince because it is too complacent. I cannot believe that the thousand heads all had happy faces or that the leaders of the Institute were all so patiently informative. A dishonest or blinkered outlook does not lead to good writing.

As with rhythm, so with diction in the evolution of modern poetry. Poets feeling that the traditional diction was stale and too facile, deliberately made their diction unpoetic; when this purge is over they are again free, if they want to, to decorate, even to use clichés (witness the poetic periphrases of Auden in some of his later poems).

A. E. Housman, who derived his poetic manner from Heine, the Border ballads, and Latin poetry, uses rhetorical tricks and clichés and blends in his diction the archaic or 'poetic' with the familiar.

For his 'poetic' diction witness:

> There flowers no balm to sain him
> From east of earth to west

or

> Tomorrow, more 's the pity, [familiar]
> Away we both must *hie*,
> To air the *ditty*,
> And to earth I. [Italics mine.]

He is fond of the grandiose hyphen: 'the sky-led seasons', 'the felon-quarried stone'. His Latin manner is shown in:

> Each in its steadfast station
> In flaming heaven they flare;
> They sign with conflagration
> The empty moors of air

and his rather affected simplicity in:

> Yes, lad, I lie easy,
> I lie as lads would choose;
> I cheer a dead man's sweetheart,
> Never ask me whose.

He writes best when he writes epigrammatically.

The early Yeats employed many 'poetic' mannerisms which he afterwards renounced. His early verse reminds us of the world of Morris's verse where everything is 'wan' and all the ladies have long

pre-Raphaelite necks. Yeats before 1899 wrote
like this:

> The love-tales wrought with silken thread
> By dreaming ladies upon cloth
> That has made fat the murderous moth;
> The roses that of old time were
> Woven by ladies in their hair,
> The dew-cold lilies ladies love
> Through many a sacred corridor. . . .

But Yeats to-day writes like this:

> Nor dread nor hope attend
> A dying animal;
> A man awaits his end
> Dreading and hoping all;
> Many times he died,
> Many times rose again.
> A great man in his pride
> Confronting murderous men
> Casts derision upon
> Supersession of breath;
> He knows death to the bone—
> Man has created death.

The early Eliot's diction is more difficult to analyse because, like parts of Joyce's *Ulysses*, it is often
a *collage* of other people's writing. Phrases and whole
sentences (and in various languages) are lifted from
other authors into his verse. (Pound in his Cantos
lifts chunks of official documents.) In such passages
naturally a study of the detailed workmanship of the
diction is as out of place as a study of brush-work in
a picture which is a *collage*. And even where Eliot's
words are his own, the diction is still often consciously
derivative (a kind of serious parody). Witness the

following, which, in its choice of words as well as in
its mood and rhythm, recalls his favourite passages
of Tourneur:

> These with a thousand small deliberations
> Protract the profit of their chilled delirium,
> Excite the membrane when the sense has cooled
> With pungent sauces, multiply variety
> In a wilderness of mirrors. . . .

In many of Eliot's early poems, however, the diction
can be isolated as Eliot's own. Here, as with his
rhythms, he compromises with everyday speech:

> The October night comes down; returning as before
> Except for a slight sensation of being ill at ease
> I mount the stairs and turn the handle of the door
> And feel as if I had mounted on my hands and knees.

Literary pastiche and diction distilled from the streets
are the means by which the early Eliot depoetized
his work. In his later verse he often employs a
grand manner which is neither parody nor self-
deprecating.

The early Pound, on the other hand, was unashamedly poetic, using archaic words and all the
Aristotelian decorations and even the second person
singular, often copying other poets, but not with the
irony of Eliot:

> In vain have I striven with my soul
>   to teach my soul to bow.
> What soul boweth
>   while in his heart art thou?

But the later Pound, like the later Yeats, is sparer
and stronger. He still uses many poetic tricks, but

not so indiscriminately. He likes grammatical inversion (mentioned somewhere by Sir Arthur Quiller-Couch as one of the chief characteristics of English poetry), asyndeton, hyphens, rare words, tags of foreign languages (an extension of Aristotle's 'strange words'), and he puts his phrases together in a *pointilliste* technique:

The silver mirrors catch the bright stones and flare,
Dawn, to our waking, drifts in the green cool light;
Dew-haze blurs, in the grass, pale ankles moving.
Beat, beat, whirr, thud, in the soft turf
        under the apple-trees,
Choros nympharum, goat-foot, with the pale foot alternate;
Crescent of blue-shot waters, green-gold in the shallows,
A black cock crows in the sea-foam. . . .

Pound, as the one-time leader of the Imagists, believes in making the part do duty for the whole, whether in description or syntax. The rapidity of movement thus attainable, the 'quick shots', to use a film term, of things in particular aspects, have been much prized by many of the younger poets, whose obscurity, as I shall show in the next chapter, is often merely due to their 'cutting'.

Thus Auden's poems, in the volume published in 1930, were written in a sort of telegraphese, the less important words such as articles and conjunctions, even demonstrative and relative pronouns, being often omitted. He was aiming thereby at an economy difficult to attain in English, which is an uninflected language. His most regular trick is asyndeton, which is still much practised by most of these poets in their eagerness not to be diffuse:

> Past victory is honour, to accept
> An island governorship, back to estates
> Explored as child; coming at last to love
> Lost publicly, found secretly again
> In private flats, admitted to a sign.

This modern verse syntax sometimes appears stilted, as when Spender writes:

> Supposing then you change
> Gestures, clamp your mind in irons,
> By boxed degrees transform into past history;
> Stand on the astringent self-created promontory,
> A Greek as simple as a water-clock,
> And let the traffic creak beneath.
> You'd live then in the tricks of dreams, you'd be
> Not living, but a walking wish, private and malicious
> As my cracked aunt, or, if blown, like a banker.

Much of Spender's writing indeed has the pedantic quality of lecture-notes; this can be a virtue when the notes do not fall apart but are held together by a strong lyrical sentiment.

As described in Chapter VI, Auden, Spender, and their fellow poets, especially Day Lewis, draw many images from the modern industrial world, its trappings and machinery. Day Lewis seems to me sometimes to force this modern imagery, applying it according to too ready-made a formula:

> Go not this road, for arc-lamps cramp
> The dawn; sense fears to take
> A mortal step, and body obeys
> An automatic brake.

But the catholic principle is right which allows him

in the same sequence of poems to use a traditional
or 'poetic' image:

> Or as a poplar, ceaselessly
> Gives a soft answer to the wind:
> Cool on the light her leaves lie sleeping
> Folding a column of sweet sound.

The catholic principle is good as long as it does not
become dilettante eclecticism; everything the poet
uses must be first *felt* as appropriate.

In the same way modern poets often use terms
borrowed from various spheres of technical writing
—psychological, scientific, or sociological. Such language is valid provided the poet is himself in a position to use it naturally and provided the ideal normal
reader can be expected to understand it. Coleridge
maintained that the philosopher comes nearer to 'the
real language of men' than the peasant. Modifying
this we may say that any language which is pruned,
concentrated, and meticulously used, tends to become
technical and that therefore it is only natural that
the poet, when looking for his 'real language', should
borrow the technical terms of other thinkers who
have already used a process of distillation similar to
the poetic one. But he must not, in tapping these
new sources, let them go to his head. Thus Auden
in his undergraduate poems overdid what he called
his 'clinical' vocabulary.

Poets are always in danger of writing to a cut-and-
dried recipe. As a child (see Chapter II) I believed
that rhyme and the use of the second person singular
were enough to make a poem. When I was at Oxford
I felt almost the same about grammatical inversion—

'Came the Dawn'—or the use of 'strange words' such as 'colubrine' or of stock poetic words, vaguely evocative, such as 'dolorous' and 'languorous'. So the undergraduate imitators of Eliot felt that a poem's success was guaranteed by broken syntax or tags of foreign languages or the mention of rats and bones. And many young poets now feel that you can make a poem with a pylon.

It is interesting to see how some even of the most 'hard-boiled' poetic experimenters rely on poetic clichés. Analysis would prove this in the work of E. E. Cummings, the 'tough-guy' American poet, who in his earlier work had two distinct manners. One manner involved the use of trick typography, drunkenly broken syntax, heaps of rather brutal slang; this manner, like Ernest Hemingway's prose, concealed an inverted sentimentality. In his other manner he was openly sentimental, employing stock poetic epithets and the second person singular, but saving his face by lack of punctuation (itself a sentimental device designed to give an effect of breathless sincerity, of flux that is only too true) and by putting odd words such as adverbs in surprising and exciting positions. This manner (as well as the other) was copied by a young English poet, Clere Parsons:

April who *dost* abet me with *shy* smiles
If I *made bold by amorous fancy* touch
Suddenly with my lips *thy* shining lips *which*
Are the smooth tulip and *chaste* crocus bulb
Lady be swift to pardon me this much. [Italics mine.]

I should not dream of demanding that poets should not have tricks. Any word is itself a trick to start with. But all tricks should be used with discrimination and delicacy of touch. We should not 'show the works' and our tricks should be suited to our subject-matter.

For this reason, we ought not now to expect to write continuously in conceits like Donne or Carew because we have not been reared either on scholastic philosophy or the periphrases of a court tradition. Nor again should we expect to use the tapestry diction of 'The Life and Death of Jason' or 'The Idyls of the King'. We are more likely to use a diction, not modelled on but parallel to, that of those poets who in lucid but dignified language have treated of contemporary life—Chaucer or Dryden or Wordsworth, or, in lighter verse, Byron.

Thus Auden can write:

> The earth turns over, our side feels the cold,
> And life sinks choking in the wells of trees;
> The ticking heart comes to a standstill, killed,
> The icing on the pond waits for the boys.
> Among the holly and the gifts I move,
> The carols on the piano, the glowing hearth,
> All our traditional sympathy with birth,
> Put by your challenge to the shifts of love.

An intricate subject will often mean a less simple diction, while certain emotions may call for more traditionally evocative words. Thus I do not agree with those critics who object to Spender for using the latter:

> high rooms of a house where voices
> Murmured at night from the garden, as if flowering from
> water.

A beloved may still be compared to a star or a rose, provided the comparison is fused with the poem and not merely 'appliquéd' on to it. Thus epithets such as 'great', 'vast', 'enormous', 'lovely', or 'beautiful' may be used, provided the general coinage is not thereby debased.

Frederic Prokosch is a poet on the border-line between the significant and the florid. In many of his early poems the exuberant use of geography suggests a child got loose with a paint-box (and he has not a contemporary reason for this, as Marlowe had). Often, too, an over-use of 'big' epithets makes the whole piece flat:

> And finally, having come to the world's long boundary
> We waited, but saw nothing; waited, but no
> Sound broke the huge stillness; and slowly turning
> Saw only stars like snow on the endless prairie
>   And a sea of snow.

But in diction, as in metric, Prokosch is a living example of the fact that architectonic can salve a traditional manner from sterile mannerism.

Our diction must have vigour, be familiar enough to be recognizable, new enough to be arresting. But vigour at the cost of lucidity or sincerity or proportion is to be avoided. Thus, though admiring it, I disapprove of the hardly intelligible synthetic Scots dialect of Hugh M'Diarmid:

> At darknin' hings abune the howff
> A weet and wild and eisenin' air.
> Spring's spirit wi' its waesome sough
> Rules owre the drucken stramash there.

And, though admitting it to be a *tour de force*, I

deplore the highfalutin of Roy Campbell (though this vice lies not only in the diction of his verse but in its movement):

> The world, revolving like a vast cocoon,
> Unwound its threading leagues at my desire:
> With burning stitches by the sun and moon
> My life was woven like a shawl of fire . . . &c.

Our diction should be masculine but not exhibitionist. After the feminine writing of most of the nineteenth century (with the exception of the lighter Byron, parts of Wordsworth and Browning) and after the neuter writing of the Georgians we are working back towards the normal virile efficiency of Dryden or Chaucer. It is significant that Eliot, for all his flux, his 'free associations', his dream-jumps, his generally passive attitude, should so much admire the writing of Dryden. As it was significant that Hopkins, with his tortured soul and tortured language, should have expressed the same admiration, even saying, 'my style tends always more towards Dryden. What is there in Dryden? Much, but above all this: he is the most masculine of our poets; his style and his rhythms lay the strongest stress of all our literature on the naked thew and sinew of the English language. . . .'

That thew and sinew are nowadays reappearing. Witness much of Auden or, on a less ambitious plane, the verse of Norman Cameron and William Plomer. And even in such an esoteric poet as Charles Madge they at times show through his coverings of astrology:

Down by the river, where the ragged are,
Continuous the cries and noise of birth,
While to the muddy edge dark fishes move

And over all, like death, or sloping hill,
Is nature, which is larger and more still.

IX

OBSCURITY[1]

THE public is always complaining that poems are obscure. When I was at Oxford any one who objected that a poem was obscure was usually told that it was only so to one who approached it with his brain; what were non sequiturs to the brain could be vindicated by a logic of the emotions or the senses. Thus one often heard that the notes to Eliot's 'Waste Land' were superfluous to an understanding of the poem. To 'get' the poem it was not necessary to know the point of its historical or literary allusions or to understand its tags of foreign languages or even to sort out who was who in it. This attitude finds a sanction in A. E. Housman's lecture on 'The Name and Nature of Poetry':

'Meaning is of the intellect, poetry is not. . . . For me the most poetical of all poets is Blake. . . . Blake's meaning is often unimportant or virtually non-existent, so that we can listen with all our hearing to his celestial tune. . . . Blake again and again, as Shakespeare now and then, gives us *poetry neat or adulterated with so little meaning* [italics mine] that nothing except poetic emotion is perceived and matters.'

The implication here that meaning is an alloy which adulterates poetry cuts the ground from under the literary critic. That would not matter so much, but it is a very dangerous doctrine for the poets them-

[1] In this chapter I am largely repeating myself, gathering up points which I have made in discussing imagery or technique.

selves, as it can be developed into the vicious extremes of pure music poetry or surrealism. I will
take these extreme cases first, for they do not really
belong to this chapter. (Obscurity must imply the
obscuration of a meaning, so that, if there is no meaning intended, it is out of place to talk of obscurity.
The surrealists and the pure music poets are above
or below obscurity as animals are above or below
immorality.)

The pure music poet is hardly ever found in practice, though some little time ago one met him frequently in theory. He is the man who puts words
together merely for the sound they make. As all
the denotations and connotations of words are to be
discounted, he is not required to keep to any of the
conventions of language. He is entitled on his premisses to make a poem entirely consisting of preposi-
tions or of invented nonsense words. His words are
phonetic cyphers. The reader meeting such a poem
need be nothing more than an ear. In answer to this
doctrine it is only necessary to say (*a*) that it is almost
impossible for poets to write poems on this principle, and (*b*) that in any case it would not be worth
doing. How long can any of us listen to poems in a
language which we do not understand? And how
differentiated are our reactions to such poems?

It should be remembered, however, that many
poets *sometimes* insert words or phrases or lines just
(or, at least, mainly) because they like the sound of
them and that such lines may often obscure their
meaning; further, that poets frequently choose, for
the sake of the sound, phrases which carry their

meaning but not as obviously as the less musical phrases to which they are preferred. There are also phrases which, as pure meaning, are less exact but, as being onomatopoeic, are more exact than the obvious ones, to which they are therefore legitimately preferred.

Surrealism is a more pernicious because a more practicable doctrine. The surrealist, in his own words, is a 'modest registering machine'. What he registers is his Unconscious. His conscious mind is not allowed (in theory, at least) either to supervise or to select. Though I suspect that if a surrealist, while dutifully not thinking what he was writing, were to register a perfectly logical syllogism, he would promptly suppress it or distort it. If the surrealists could confine themselves to being modest registering machines, they would do useful spadework for the psychologists. But I have not enough faith in the modesty of human beings to believe that the surrealists work within their own limits.

The surrealist, then, has more meaning than the pure music poet, but his meaning is not of the surface. To get at his meaning we must not ask what he is driving at, for he is not driving at anything; he is modestly registering. Technique means nothing to him. It is we who have to do his analysis for him—to sort out his symbols for Sex, for the Womb, for Death. This is not necessarily difficult, because many surrealists tend to use the stock symbols acquired from the psychological text-books. But, if they are conscious of these symbols as symbols, it is very possible that their Unconscious has withdrawn to some farther Hindenburg line which they cannot reach. In my opinion, in order to give a chance to the Unconscious, the writer should leave it alone and fix his conscious mind on a manifest subject.

Hear the surrealists speak for themselves, in *The First Manifesto of Surrealism* (1924):

'Surrealism, as I envisage it, displays our complete *non-conformity* so clearly that there can be no question of claiming it as witness when the real world comes up for trial. On the contrary, it can but testify to the complete state of distraction to which we hope to attain here below. . . . Surrealism is the "invisible ray" that shall enable us one day to overcome our enemies. . . . This summer the roses are blue; the wood is made of glass. The earth wrapped in its foliage makes as little effect on me as a ghost. Living and ceasing to live are imaginary solutions. Existence is elsewhere.'

If existence is elsewhere, art, we may add, is elsewhere also. Schizophrenia and paranoia may be, as the Freudians suggest, parallel to and alternative to art; they are not identical with it. I agree with Christopher Caudwell's statement in 'Illusion and Reality' —'it is also the character of surréalisme, as it is the character of anarchy as a political philosophy, that it *negates itself in practice*'. (For Caudwell, surrealism is, after Parnassianism, Symbolism, &c., the 'logical extreme development of "art for art's sake"—i.e. "art for my sake" '.)

We must remember, however, that just as many more conventional poets at moments approximate to the pure music poet, so at moments (as Coleridge in 'Kubla Khan') they approximate to the surrealist. Thus modern poetry is full of 'free association'. But when the poet is consciously selecting his 'free

associations', as Joyce does in *Ulysses*, he is not properly surrealist. It should be easiest to write surrealist
poetry when drunk or in a state of hypnosis. Thus
many surrealist poems remind one of a drunk man
talking (or of the spiritualist medium's child-talk),
but, like the drunk man's maunderings, they often
have a strain of sense in them. (After all there are
also *ideas* in the Unconscious.)

Thus, in a translation of a poem by Georges
Hugnet:

Your face does not exist,
my love is well polished,
the sea interrogates its beaches secretly,
living is not following a mirror's movements as best one can,
the winged ant is an ear,
tears are the beggars who roll to the bottoms of ponds,
a room is the bother of leaving it . . .

the attention is only held because tantalized by several
incipient meanings. Thus line 3 might be one of
the pathetic fallacies employed in ordinary romantic
poetry, line 4 might be a romantic restatement of a
maxim of La Rochefoucauld, line 5 is pure nonsense,
line 6 might be a Hans Andersen fairy story *in parvo*,
line 7 could be regarded as a wittily condensed philosophical paradox, a definition by negation, to be explained thus: a room, as Aristotle would say, is only
a room if it is a room for people to go into (as Aristotle denies that a dead hand is a hand); therefore
it is the fact that people cannot do without rooms—
cannot leave them for good—which maintains their
status as rooms.

Most surrealists use no syntax or punctuation be-

cause the essence of their work is that it should be
fortuitous. Now the fortuitous tends to be boring;
I am quite unmoved by the famous example from
Lautréamont of 'the chance meeting, on a dissecting-
table, of a sewing-machine and an umbrella'. The
poet needs to narrow his sphere. As everything may
in the long run be relevant to everything else, there
may always be a significance in the chance meeting
of *x* and *y* on *z*. And, nearer home, there is always
the possibility of comic relief in the juxtaposition of
the unexpected. But the Unexpected does not wear
well. We cannot make it the basis for poetry any more
than we can make the practical joke a basis for con-
duct. F. H. Bradley in his 'Logic' states that every
judgement is ultimately a judgement about the uni-
verse. But this does not mean that one judgement is
not more important or more correct than another (in
idealist philosophies, so often, we cannot see the
trees for the wood). The poet, like the practical
man, must presuppose a scale of values. Any odd
set of words which any one uses may, on ultimate
analysis, be significant, but the poet cannot wait for
this ultimate. And, if he could, why should he
bother to be a poet, seeing that the idiots in their
institutions, the babies in their prams, can be just
as significant without effort?

I have compared the surrealist to a drunk man.
Now some drunks are more lucid, or at least more
suggestive, in their conversation than others, and I
have met poems, apparently written on surrealist
principles, which could hold the attention, thanks
either to a more delicate selectiveness (conscious or

unconscious) on the author's part or to his verbal sense (a thing which on surrealist principles counts for nothing). A good example is Dylan Thomas, who is very obscure and incoherent, but at least more human than the official surrealists; one can sometimes get into touch with him. He is like a drunk man speaking wildly but rhythmically, pouring out a series of nonsense images, the cumulative effect of which is usually vital and sometimes even seems to have a message—this message being adolescence, the discovery of the power and horror of sex and so of all the changes in nature, *natura naturans*. The statements as statements are nonsense, but it is obvious what his mind is drunkenly running on:

> A candle in the thighs
> Warms youth and seed and burns the seeds of age;
> Where no seed stirs,
> The fruit of man unwrinkles in the stars,
> Bright as a fig;
> Where no wax is, the candle shows its hairs.

To come now to those poets who would not admit that they write like drunks or madmen, or even like singing birds. Much of their poetry also is difficult to understand, though they themselves are writing with clear heads. Is their obscurity good or bad, necessary or affected?

Sometimes, undoubtedly, it is affected and bad. Witness most of the poems in *Transition* or in *Active Anthology*, an anthology edited by Ezra Pound of work by his imitators. The word 'cryptic' means 'concealing something'; most of these poems are like boxes with a hidden lock—if, and when, you find the lock, there is nothing inside; all that was concealed was the lock and not the contents. Much cryptic poetry, however, has got things inside it. Witness Rilke, Eliot, Yeats, the early Auden.

Poems can be difficult because of their subject-matter or because of their form. Difficult subject-matter may be either objective or subjective. Thus a didactic poem about the theories of Einstein would be difficult and so would a 'private' poem about one's own inner history which the public does not know. On the other hand, the subject of a poem may be familiar and generally comprehensible, but may be expressed in a manner which disguises this meaning. On analysis, however, such disguise is only legitimate if this subject, familiar and comprehensible to the public, has for the poet certain modifications, overtones, outside references, or implicit contradictions, which turn it into a far more intricate subject than it appeared at first sight, into a subject which itself requires an intricate handling. For example, suppose I am in love. Well and good; that sounds much simpler than Einstein. But suppose my love is tortured, ambiguous, sporadic, complicated, connected in my mind with all sorts of things outside itself. In that case I must not simply say 'I am in love' without qualifying it. It would be honest of me to add that my love is ambiguous, sporadic, complicated, &c. But I might find that *poetically* I could convey the total effect better by tampering with the form of the poem, making the verse itself sympathetic to its subject—tortured or sporadic or complicated. This is a dangerous principle if applied too consciously, but is a principle which has often affected poets' form.

Much of the obscurity of modern poetry is to be referred to its 'cutting'—to borrow a term from the cinema. Many modern poets leave out those links between idea and idea or between image and image which earlier poets would have inserted. They do this (*a*) for the sake of speed and concentration (it must be remembered that a conjunction, like a gate, is also disjunctive), and (*b*) because they wish to convey the broken pattern, the quick transitions of their own thoughts or lives or worlds. (It is no prejudice for or against our period which makes me say that for most people now the world comes quicker upon them, both in respect of material speed—modern transport, factories, American hustle—and in respect of the vast distances which have to be covered if the mind is to keep up with the sheer knowledge, general, specialized or technical, that has now been accumulated. By buying a newspaper we can acquire more new facts—for what they are worth—in a day than a Greek poet could in a month.)

The corresponding Americanization of poetry was accordingly introduced to England by Americans— Eliot and Pound, who were all for complexity and speed, for snaps of the moving pattern. Thus Eliot wrote in 1917 (in an essay on 'Tradition and the Individual Talent'): 'The poet's mind is . . . a receptacle for seizing and storing up numberless feelings, phrases, images, which remain there until all the particles which can unite to form a new compound are present together.' [Like a motor-car factory where the chassis slides past 'impersonally' on its platform until all its body is fitted on to it. Eliot, remember, is an addict to 'impersonality'.] Again, in 1921, in an essay on 'The Metaphysical Poets', Eliot wrote:

'When a poet's mind is perfectly equipped for its work, it is constantly amalgamating disparate experience; the ordinary man's experience is chaotic, irregular, fragmentary. The latter falls in love, or reads Spinoza [it is typical of Eliot that his ordinary man should read Spinoza], and these two experiences have nothing to do with each other, or with the noise of the typewriter or the smell of cooking; in the mind of the poet these experiences are always forming new wholes.'

Eliot's earlier poems are mainly written to the formula of Spinoza and the smell of cooking. It is not surprising that the ordinary man, who cannot, as Eliot says, correlate these ingredients in life, failed to correlate them when he first met them in poetry, especially as Eliot's new whole was not unified for him by traditional versification. It is to be noted, however, that Eliot's early poems are now much 'easier' than they were ten years ago. People have been trained to follow him, just as they have been trained to follow quickly moving films.

The extreme example of this method is Ezra Pound's Cantos. Here Pound takes the whole of history as stock for his soup and cuts backwards and forwards from one country or one century to another, adding plenty of the smell of cooking and noise of the typewriter to make it clear that all these elements combine for him in a living and contemporary whole. I doubt if they will so combine for many of his

readers. In a poem on so large a scale the method
palls and Pound's bits of history and culture are so
diverse and so particular as to fail to arouse many
echoes. This huge poem is to consist of a hundred
cantos. In Canto I we meet Circe out of the 'Odyssey'.
In Canto II we have the metamorphosis of Dionysus
from Ovid. In Canto III we switch to Renaissance
Italy and to the Spain of the Cid. In Canto IV we
have a mixture of Ancient China, Ancient Greece,
and the Provence of the Troubadours. For this enormous work Pound uses the method of the imagists,
and this sometimes gives effective vignettes:

> And the ship like a keel in ship-yard,
>   slung like an ox in smith's sling,
> Ribs stuck fast in the ways,
>   grape-cluster over pin-rack,
>   void air taking pelt.

But more often his passion for the particular detail
conduces to a total blur; witness those cantos which
would demonstrate apparently the economics of
Renaissance Italy:

1622 January, assigned on the Paschi
Off° de Paschi
March 1622 Donna Orsola of wherever removed from the
    book of
the Sienese public women (motion approved by the Bailey). . . .

For the Eliot-Pound method allows of the bodily
transference into a poem not only of tags from other
poetry or prose but of bits of public records, washing-
bills, statistics. Sometimes, as in 'The Waste Land',
such ingredients blend successfully, fused together

by an intense lyrical theme, but on the whole I consider this method to be vicious. The poem tends
to remain heterogeneous and therefore bad. Thus
Eliot's 'Triumphal March'—another shuffling of
past and present history, of Caesar and the twentieth
century—is fatally broken up by a prose catalogue
of armaments:

> 5,800,000 rifles and carbines,
> 102,000 machine guns &c.

Some of Eliot's early poems can be called impressionist, in the way that the first half of *Ulysses* is impressionist. Thus in 'Rhapsody on a Windy Night'
after mentioning a woman the corner of whose eye

> Twists like a crooked pin

Eliot goes on recording realistically the 'free associations' of a tired man at midnight

> The memory throws up high and dry
> A crowd of twisted things;
> A twisted branch upon the beach
> Eaten smooth, and polished
> As if the world gave up
> The secret of its skeleton,
> Stiff and white.
> A broken spring in a factory yard,
> Rust that clings to the form that the strength has left
> Hard and curled and ready to snap.

Such writing corresponds to common experience
and is only difficult because people tend to forget
such of their experiences as they cannot label, experiences which are not pertinent to any course of
action. But now that psycho-analysis insists on people

remembering their idle thoughts and sensations, or their thoughts and sensations in dreams, this kind of impressionism is recognized as valid.

Eliot's next book of 'Poems' (1920) is difficult because here Eliot is being the witty man of culture. He cuts quickly not by the impressionist method of free association but by juxtaposing shots of the contemporary world with shots which he has deliberately hoarded and selected from his world of books or culture:

The horses under the axle-tree
  Beat up the dawn from Istria   [Graeco-Roman image of
                                     the sun.]
With even feet. Her shuttered barge   [Cleopatra.]
  Burned on the water all the day.

But this or such was Bleistein's way:
  A saggy bending of the knees
And elbows with the palms turned out
  Chicago Semite Viennese.

In 'The Waste Land' (1922) Eliot produced a longer poem on the decay of Western civilization—the disappearance of religion, the depreciation of sex. The manner is again mosaic—sometimes psychologically impressionist, sometimes consciously eclectic. The key-line to 'The Waste Land' is 'These fragments I have shored against my ruins' (itself a fragment of Kyd), and Eliot's technique is suited to his matter, the verse is fragmentary. But this, as I said, is a dangerous principle, and 'The Waste Land' is a bad model for poets. And its subject, as I said (see the quotation from Matthew Arnold on page 13), is a subject to be rarely treated; it comes too near nihilism. 'The Waste Land' is like snatches of overheard conversation—several people talking at once and some of them ghosts—and also like very intricate music in which motifs reappear for a bar or two and are promptly submerged. It is obscure because of its cutting, because of its many erudite allusions, because it is strung on the very specialized theme of a book by Miss Jessie Weston, because its pictures, like dream pictures, are given without qualification.

Sometimes, in his earlier poems, Eliot was difficult through a kind of metaphysical wit. Some people are puzzled even by examples which seem to me lucid—'The smoky candle-end of time Declines', or 'I have measured out my life with coffee spoons'. This latter line, which a friend of mine told me he could not understand, is surely a memorably epigrammatic way of saying: My life has been trivial, full of non-significant social engagements, strung on an empty routine.

But since 'The Waste Land' Eliot's poems have become more positively religious and so have contained more metaphysical writing in the wider sense:

> Shape without form, shade without colour,
> Paralysed force, gesture without motion . . .

and this desire to put, poetically, religious or philosophical paradoxes has even hardened into a kind of mannerism of antithesis or oxymoron:

> All our knowledge brings us nearer to our ignorance,
> All our ignorance brings us nearer to death,
> But nearness to death no nearer to God.
> Where is the Life we have lost in living?
> Where is the wisdom we have lost in knowledge?
> Where is the knowledge we have lost in information?

Thus his most recent poem, 'Burnt Norton', a poem about time, has as its key-phrase 'the still point of the turning world'. Eliot's cutting is still bold, but the difficulty here lies in the thought itself.

On the whole, however, the famous obscurity of Eliot can be referred to his technique, but his technique in turn can be referred to his subject-matter, that is to Eliot's own world and so to Eliot himself. Eliot is a person of exceptional book-learning, for whom, as he says himself of Donne, an idea is really an experience and who does tend to bring in Spinoza when he hears the noise of the typewriter. It is not wrong of Eliot to be difficult, because Eliot would be posing if he were easy. Eliot, for all his adherence to the Anglican Church, is essentially one of the few. I suspect that Eliot is bound to be a rather esoteric poet because, though he may be soaked in communal traditions and communal institutions, he really is more interested in ideas on the one hand and sense-impressions on the other—Spinoza and smells—than in concrete life or the concrete human being.

Yeats, too, is a poet of the library. He believes, as already mentioned, in the Mask, the poet's pose. His world, like Hölderlin's or Rimbaud's or Rilke's, is largely a private world. He does not, as George Moore complained, look round him as he walks in the streets; consequently, when he does notice something, he may attach to it an inordinate importance. He has a private meaning to attach to everything. To pin down these private meanings the reader would not only have to know, say, the Christian Cabbala, the Bhagavadgita, ancient Irish folk-lore, and modern spiritualist doctrine, but would have to recognize Yeats's fluctuating distortions and amalgamations of these. (For example, Yeats is almost alone in regarding the early Ionian philosophers as mystics rather than scientists.) In Yeats, however, the reader is helped along by logical syntax and a recognizable metric. Yeats's sound is so good that many readers do not bother about the precise meaning; they get a general impression of other-worldliness, of a mystical faith, of an attitude to the passage of time. But if we examine the poems in 'The Tower' we find that the Tower is both the real stone tower owned by Yeats in Co. Galway and an intellectual symbol—sometimes 'emblematical of the night' (and the night is emblematical of something else), sometimes representing the aspirations of strong individuals:

> A bloody, arrogant power
> Rose out of the race
> Uttering, mastering it,
> Rose like these walls from these
> Storm-beaten cottages. . . .

When we leave Eliot or Pound or Yeats and come to Auden or Spender, we enter a more vulgar world. (The vulgarity in Eliot is always carefully put in its place *as* vulgarity.) These younger poets are less conditioned by culture and more concerned with life *as they live it*. (None of them, incidentally, has followed a purely literary profession. Spender has never had a job, but has given much time to political work.) Where Eliot insists that the poet should be an observer, impersonal, looking at the stream from the bank, these younger poets do not cut off their

poetic activity from their activity in general. Being
'personal' poets, then, their obscurity will be of a
different kind from that of Eliot or from that of the
modestly registering surrealists, also from that of
the 'personal' poet, Yeats, for personality for them
does not imply such utter individualism.

Both Auden and Spender have written much which
is obscure. Their obscurity *is* like Eliot's in that
they regularly try to form wholes out of disparate
experiences and ideas. But it is unlike Eliot's in that
they select such experiences and ideas by criteria
taken from actual life. Thus Spender in his more
personal lyrics might bring in both Spinoza and the
smell of cooking, but these would be ancillary to the
personal emotion governing the poem. And Auden
in his campaigning poems might bring in almost anything, but it would be introduced not as pure impressionism but in order to support or illustrate a thesis.

Readers found Auden's first book of 'Poems'
(1930) very difficult indeed. This was partly because
these poems were full of ideas, and ideas at that
borrowed from the fields of anthropology, say, or
psychology or the preciser sciences, from Groddeck
or Homer Lane, and thrown at the reader as if he
were already familiar with them. Secondly, these ideas
were not very carefully co-ordinated; Auden has
always been rather slapdash in construction. Thirdly,
as already described, Auden in these poems used a
peculiar technique, a kind of telegraphese. Instead,
for example, of saying 'We can speak of trouble' or
'One can speak of trouble' he would start straight off
with the verb 'Can speak of trouble'.

Sometimes, apart from the meaning being technical, these poems were difficult because the thought was intricate:

> Love by ambition
> Of definition
> Suffers partition
> And cannot go
> From yes to no. . . .

Auden at that time was fascinated by the subtleties of Graves, Laura Riding, and Emily Dickinson. The influence of Graves is clearly shown when he writes:

> Sentries against inner and outer
> At stated interval is feature. . . .

Sometimes the difficulty was merely rhetorical. Thus the later Auden has adopted the Dantesque periphrasis—'to the east the neat man who ordered Gorki to be electrified' [equals Lenin].

Sometimes he sacrifices lucidity jointly for the sake of concentration and pattern. Witness an early example:

> Is first baby, warm in mother,
> Before born and is still mother,
> Time passes and now is other,
> Is knowledge in him now of other,
> Cries in cold air, himself no friend.
> In grown man also, may see in face
> In his day-thinking and in his night-thinking
> Is wareness and is fear of other,
> Alone in flesh, himself no friend.

This at first sight is highly ambiguous; 'first baby' might mean a first baby as distinct from a second

baby; 'before born' might mean one that had been
born before, and so on. These lines could be translated lucidly into prose (though the result would
not be emotionally so effective; the echoing end-
words, the refrain of 'himself no friend', convey to
me a feeling of forlorn necessity). But a prose explanation would be: before birth a man is identified
with his mother, secure in the womb; birth, in the
Freudian phrase, is a great, perhaps the greatest,
trauma; the man knows himself as a separate
individual, but *ipso facto* knows himself as an incom-
plete individual; he therefore requires, to replace his
mother, a life complementary to his own—the Aristotelian Alter Ego; but he is terrified of the candidates
for this position.

Auden's view of the world encourages him to use
certain words in specialized senses. For example,
he sometimes seems to use the word 'ghost' to denote
either hereditary influence or a man's own slant backwards towards his parents or ancestors. Auden has
always been much occupied with the paradoxes of
family relationships. And in general his thought
involves many paradoxes, such as are put more explicitly in the theses of psychologists or philosophers,
for example, the observation that the apparently
courageous are really cowards or, at least, that their
courage is the flower of their cowardice:

One staring too long, went blind in a tower.
One sold all his manors to fight, *broke through, and faltered.*
[Italics mine.]

Auden being so interested in the phenomenon of the
man of action (for example, in Colonel Lawrence),

many of his lyrics contain in a condensed form what
is worked out at length in the play, *The Ascent of
F6*—the tragedy of the man who gets his own way.
But Auden, while regarding so many of our neuroses
as tragic, so many of our actions as self-deception,
yet believes, as I have already said, that neurosis is
the cause of an individual's development. Such a
psychological dialectic reflects itself in the paradoxes
and the tension of his poems.

Spender's poems similarly are often difficult because the meaning itself is intricate, though this
intricacy is not due so much as in Auden to an
adaptation or syncretism of specialist-theories, but
rather to Spender's own very equivocal view of the
world in which he lives. In speaking of imagery I
suggested that Spender's images pull more than their
own weight, tend to become as factual as his properties. And many things in his poems seem, like Yeats's
Tower, to exist on two planes of reality at once. Thus
in his poem 'The North', put into the mouth of explorers, the North is not only the actual north defined by latitude, but is a symbol of negation both
of time and of ordinary values (as no doubt it may
sometimes seem to explorers themselves; compare
Moby Dick, where the white whale is so much more
than a whale). And Spender's poem, 'Alas for the
Sad Standards', is a 'metaphysical' comparison of
young men killed in battle to the pictures of old
masters, the lives of both being removed from us,
become static, fixed at a point. The parallel is
strengthened by a conceit, the glazed eyes of the
dead being compared to the glass and the glaze of

varnish which come between us and the pictures—
an important conceit because Spender is emphasizing
the *transparent* wall which separates us from the
dead:

> Through glass their eyes meet ours
> Like standards of the masters
> That shock us with their peace.

[Notice the dispersed oxymoron of the last line.]

Spender's view of the world, as I said, is equivocal
—but honest. Adopting Marxist doctrine he yet sym-
pathizes with the Anarchists and this poetic anarch-
ism glosses his writing with fantasy. Compare a
novel, which Spender very much admires, Ramon
Sender's *Seven Red Sundays*.

Fewer poets nowadays write obscurely for the
Symbolist reason that obscurity is delightful in itself. In examining my own poems I find that, when
they are obscure, it is either because my meaning is
complicated or because, while having a clear meaning, I consent to compromise its lucid expression for
the sake of a gain in speed, concentration, colour, or
the music of the verse. Occasionally I am recording
facts which belong to dream rather than waking, but,
unlike the surrealists proper, I do not record these
automatically. Thus in a poem called 'Perseus', presenting an experience and a mood from which I have
often suffered, I write:

Or look in the looking-glass in the end room—
You will find it full of eyes,
The ancient smiles of men cut out with scissors and kept in
    mirrors.

To put this more explicitly would disperse the atmosphere of dream. I am describing a mood of terror when everything seems to be unreal, petrified—hence the Gorgon's head, which dominates this poem. Such a mood being especially common among children, 'the end room' implies a child's fear of long corridors. In such a mood, both when a child and when grown-up, I remember looking in mirrors and (*a*) thinking that my own face looked like a strange face, especially in the eyes, and (*b*) being fascinated and alarmed by the mysterious gleams of light *glancing* off the mirror. And, lastly, a mirror is a symbol of nihilism via solipsism.

If a poet is asked why he should not take more words to explain what his fewer words leave obscure, the answer often is that if the experience to be conveyed was itself a unity, this unity will be broken up by discursive treatment (otherwise such an experience could even be conveyed in prose). I give another example of condensation from my own poems, which I have often been told is obscure. A poem called 'Hidden Ice', in praise of ordinary people who live by routine, ends with these two verses:

But some though buoyed by habit, though convoyed
By habitual faces and hands that help the food
Or help one with one's coat, have lost their bearings
Struck hidden ice or currents no one noted.

One was found like Judas kissing flowers
And one who sat between the clock and the sun
Lies like a Saint Sebastian full of arrows
Feathered from his own hobby, his pet hours.

The meaning of the first of these verses is clear. The second verse gives examples of the people who strike hidden ice, members of the routine world who fall away from their allegiance. They are persons who become unable to keep their aesthetic sense or their outside interests or their erotic emotions pigeon-holed off into the hours when they are not on duty. They become obsessed by something which, on their system, should not be allowed to intrude into their eight-hour day. They kiss flowers and like Judas because the act is treacherous to their whole system (it is also implied that these 'flowers', as Christ to Judas, are themselves potentially destructive of the system. Witness the routine worker who becomes a Communist). And some of these people become *fatally* addicted to what belongs, on their premises, to their pet hours only. Such people in everyday life may end in suicide or the asylum. Such a man is like Saint Sebastian because his collapse is brought about through the things he loved—the arrow in his body feathered from the birds which he himself reared. ('Hobby' is an ironic understatement; for a man who is a mere cog in industry or business, any love or any ideal must be a hobby.) As for sitting 'between the clock and the sun', this denotes sitting between the two great symbols of routine, one human and the other natural. Further, both a clock ticking and a shaft of sun entering a room (the dust-motes dancing in it corresponding to the inevitable ticking of the clock) seem to me, at moments, sinister, hypnotic. And—a minor point—the sun enters the room at the time when the malingerer ought to be at his work. Further, I am not merely using clock and sun as symbols, for I have a clear picture of a particular man with suicidal thoughts sitting in a room with a clock on the mantelpiece behind him and the sun creeping towards him over the floor from a window in front.

On the whole, modern poetry is becoming more lucid, and that because its subject is less esoteric. The suggestions of the Symbolists may still be occasionally used, but for an end outside themselves. On the other hand, rhetoric (which the Symbolists banned) will be used, as by Auden, but similarly not for its own sake—not as it was used by so many Latin poets. True rhetoric presupposes a certain scale of values, certain conceptions of good and evil. Such a scale of values, however uncertain and fluctuating, is implicit in the poetry of Auden and Spender. Their poetry may be expected to become clearer side by side with their philosophy, provided the public itself becomes at home with such philosophy.

X

LIGHTER POETRY AND DRAMA

i

THE poet, as I have said, is a specialist in something which every one practises. Every one practises love-talk, and the poet distils from this something which through its shape and balance will more than compensate for the lack of the spoken word, the tones of the voice. But every one also practises trivial talk, humorous talk, joke-talk, and these varieties also should be represented on the poetic plane. It is vicious to demand that poetry should always be concerned with 'beauty' (in the narrower sense, for a good joke is beautiful) or uplift or intense emotion.

Modern critics have been too exclusively concerned with the lyric. Some have even suggested that no long poem can be all poetry because a poem is essentially a crystal unit. This is nonsense. Chaucer is poetry; the Odyssey (though Colonel Lawrence denied it) is poetry; even the Epistles of Horace are poetry. And Wordsworth in his contacts with his 'flesh and blood' never made complete contact because he lacked a sense of humour.

The lighter sides of the human animal should be represented in verse as well as his 'high seriousness'. But as his lighter elements are themselves alloyed, to varying degrees, with seriousness, poetry can show every kind of blend of lightness and seriousness. Some intensely serious poetry has a streak of lightness in it, while there is little 'light verse' which has not a serious undertone, however tiny. Thus many of the Odes of Horace could be classed as light verse, yet it is difficult to deny that they are serious, that they reflect a serious and sincere attitude to life.

Every one is at times cynical or irritated or frivolous or good humouredly or bad humouredly critical or whimsical or lightly philosophical or merely full of animal high spirits. Such common and natural moods find their expression in the lighter kinds of poetry. I have already explained why so much serious poetry is melancholy; conversely, when one writes from happiness or gaiety one may often be expected to write lightly. This is not to say that some light verse—witness the 'Dunciad'—does not originate partly, or indeed largely, in feelings of bitterness.

The two poles of lighter poetry are the 'Grain of Salt' and the 'Urge to Nonsense'. These can be roughly correlated with my previous, carefully qualified distinction between 'Criticism of Life' and 'Escape'. Pure satire would be an expression of the former, pure nonsense verse of the latter. But it is rare to meet with either pure satire or pure nonsense. Much nonsense verse, such as Lear's, conceals genuine emotional reactions to the writer's life and world, while, on the other hand, much satire is written for the fun of it rather than as pure criticism (thus Juvenal was primarily a rhetorician who would have liked to write epic but took up satire as a substitute opportunity for fine writing). Freud, in his book on Wit, has argued that many lampoons or epigrams at some one's expense are merely fastened on to 'some one' who provides an opportunity for the childish instinct for play, for pattern.[1] The differentia of a lampoon, then, would not be its polemical content, but the peculiarly attractive pattern for which such a content is an occasion.

In most lighter verse the 'Grain of Salt' and the 'Urge to Nonsense' are blended. For example, the magnificent Irish ballad 'Johnny, I hardly knew ye' is on the face of it just a normally light-hearted ballad on the subject of war, but why this ballad has such peculiar appeal is, I think, partly because it contains a sardonic criticism of war typical of the hardened cynicism which familiarity with war breeds in ordinary people. Lighter love lyrics, such as George Wither's 'I loved a lass, a fair one', contain a certain minimum of reference to actual love, but are really nonsense or escape poems. This is always a favourite type among popular songs.

If we look at the world's literature, we see that much of the richness of life is represented in poetry which would be excluded by those critics who are more interested in poetry's dignity or narrowness. Aristophanes gives a magnificent blend of the 'Grain of Salt' and the 'Urge to Nonsense'. Catullus, admitted to be one of the greatest love-poets, uses the same technique and expresses, but enhances, the same

[1] Thus *Gulliver's Travels* is primarily a *critical* work, but the fantasy also is delighted in for its own sake.

personality in his gaily impudent lampoons. (I suspect that even some of his love-poems proper contain the grain of salt.) Ovid performs the serious and valuable function of representing frivolously a frivolous society. Villon, who reaches high poetry when lamenting man's mortality, balances this with his talent for throwing mud.

And, if we look at our own literature, we see how exceptionally rich it is in the many different kinds of lighter poetry, ranging from the humour of Chaucer at one end to the merely witty limerick at the other. Consider the Aristotelian *mimesis* of 'lower' charac- ters—the 'Wife of Bath'; the buffoonery of Skelton, who had method in his madness, or of Dunbar; Herrick's dainty homage to trivialities; Shakespeare's high spirits and nonsense:

> The lark, that tirra-lirra chants,
>> With heigh! with heigh! the thrush and the jay,
> Are summer songs for me and my aunts,
>> While we lie tumbling in the hay.

Even Milton has his playful or frivolous moments in 'L'Allegro' and 'Comus'. And consider the bludgeon satire of Marvell on the Dutch, the rapier satire of Pope, and Dryden's who comes half-way between these; the flamboyant polemic of Burns, 'Holy Willie's Prayer'; the airy narrative of Byron's 'Don Juan' or the slapstick satirical fantasy of his 'Vision of Judgment'. Or consider even the poetry of conceits, such as Carew's lines on 'A Fly that flew into my Mistress' Eye'—a legitimate genre, at any rate in its period. Or consider the extraordinary little squib poems of Blake—extremely funny, but with the lyrical intensity of some one writing with his heart in it:

> When Sir Joshua Reynolds died
> All nature was degraded;
> The King dropp'd a tear into the Queen's ear
> And all his pictures faded.

The Victorian era was comparatively barren in lighter poetry—at least among professional poets. (The Music Halls and the Street Ballad-makers picked up what the professionals ignored.) But towards the end of the Victorian era there came with Carroll and Lear the great efflorescence of nonsense verse. This nonsense poetry stands to the light verse of Pope or Swift or Praed or the lighter Byron much as poets of the Romantic Revival (including the Byron of 'Manfred') stood to their serious predecessors. Lear's nonsense poetry is the last flare-up of romanticism. His poem about himself—'How pleasant to know Mr. Lear'—shows the counterpart of the arrogant self-pity of Byron or Baudelaire. Compare:

> When he walks in a waterproof white,
>   The children run after him so!
> Calling out, 'He's come out in his night-
>   Gown, that crazy old Englishman, oh!

with

> Le Poète est semblable au prince des nuées
> Qui hante la tempête et se rit de l'archer;
> Exilé sur le sol au milieu des huées,
> Ses ailes de géant l'empêchent de marcher.

In the present century, starting with Belloc and Chesterton, light verse has grown more frequent and

wider in its range. Chesterton excelled both in nonsense and in polemic—witness his attack on F. E.
Smith. But on a higher plane poetry had already
appeared, which, like the Odes of Horace, exhibited
what Mr. Eliot, in speaking of Catullus, called an
'intense levity'. Witness many of the poems of A. E.
Housman. Housman often uses a trim little hymn-
tune form to put out his tongue at life or convention;
this is sometimes almost parody:

> Ho, every one that thirsteth
>   And hath the price to give,
> Come to the stolen waters,
>   Drink and your soul shall live.

And many of his early poems show the ironic levity
of Heine. But Housman is at his best when his
manner approximates to the popular ballad (tempered with a donnish wit):

> O, who is that young sinner with the handcuffs on his wrists?
> And what has he been after that they groan and shake their
>   fists?
> And wherefore is he wearing such a conscience-stricken air?
> O, they're taking him to prison for the colour of his hair.

or the magnificent poem beginning 'The stars have
not dealt me the worse they can do'. This ballad
manner, this vulgar approach, used by Housman,
Kipling, Chesterton, is now again being used by
poets like Auden who draw not only upon folk poetry
and broadsheets but upon the words of contemporary
jazz songs.

But, before Auden had dared to be vulgar, some
of the best light verse of the day was the rather joy-
less wit-verse of Eliot.

Witness Aunt Helen:

> Now when she died there was silence in heaven
> And silence at her end of the street.

or the Sweeney poems or 'A Cooking Egg':

> I shall not want Honour in Heaven
>   For I shall meet Sir Philip Sidney
> And have talk with Coriolanus
>   And other heroes of that kidney.
>
> I shall not want Capital in Heaven
>   For I shall meet Sir Alfred Mond,
> We two shall lie together, lapt
>   In a five per cent. Exchequer Bond.

or the ironically pompous 'Mr. Eliot's Sunday Morning Service':

> The sable presbyters approach
> The avenue of penitence;
> The young are red and pustular
> Clutching piaculative pence.

On the whole Eliot's humour is the humour of a don.

In the decade after the War the three Sitwells were writing much escape verse of the nonsense variety. This sometimes merged into satire, attacks on the middle classes, the older generation. Much bric-à-brac gave this verse an air of modernity, though allowing for the change from a studied openness (enthusiasm for 'a thousand pots of beer') to a studied artificiality, the mood is often the whimsical, sentimental mood of Rupert Brooke. Thus compare with Brooke's best poem, 'Fish', the following lines from Osbert Sitwell's 'Church-Parade':

The terrace glitters hard and white
Bedaubed and flecked with points of light
That flicker at the passers by—
Reproachful as a curate's eye.

Edith Sitwell was technically more adventurous and some of her earlier poems, especially those in Bucolic Comedies, have the charm and glitter of sophisticated nursery rhymes, jazzed up by a modern balletomane.

Light poetry, however, was more truly represented in this period by the popular light verse of the dance-hall and the music-hall, where sentimentality was at least not disguised (witness songs like the 'Blue Room') and where the age-old cynical reaction to sex was represented without any donnish pomposity.

I'm bringing her a di'mond stone,
I'll take it back when I go home.

And the 'naughty' verses of Douglas Byng or, more lately of Cole Porter did full critical justice to the world of cocktail bars and night clubs.

Some, however, of the serious poets had their own peculiar humour, with which at moments they expressed more lightly exactly the same attitude that dominated their main work. Thus even Yeats deviates at times towards nonsense, but towards a nonsense which smacks of the Cabbala:

Great Europa played the fool
That changed her lover for a bull.
Fol de rol, fol de rol.

But a more notable example is that of D. H. Law-rence, whose one and only theme produced, beside his more serious work, the free verse squibs of

Pansies and the very charming, slightly whimsical, poems about *Birds, Beasts and Flowers*, for example, of the bat which he shook out of the window:

And now, at evening, as he flickers over the river
Dipping with petty triumphant flight, and tittering over the
  sun's departure,
I believe he chirps, pipistrello, seeing me here on this terrace
  writing:
There he sits, the long loud one!
But I am greater than he. . . .
I escaped him. . . .

A dainty, contemplative whimsicality, centred on domestic objects, is shown in this period in the poems of John Crowe Ransom in America and of the early Graves in England. These poems are seriously intended and not thought of by their authors as escapist (Graves in his early critical writings used to argue that nursery rhymes or the nonsense poems of Lear were as serious, as 'true', as the tragedies of Shakespeare). Witness Ransom's poem, 'Janet Waking', on a little girl and the death of her pet hen:

> It was a transmogrifying bee
> Came droning down on Chucky's old bald head
> And sat and put the poison. It scarcely bled,
> But how exceedingly
>
> And purply did the knot
> Swell with the venom and communicate
> Its rigour! Now the poor comb stood up straight
> But Chucky did not.

These two poets brought a metaphysical attitude into the nursery. Graves, from writing straight colourful nursery rhymes:

Henry was a worthy king,
   Mary was his queen.
He gave to her a snowdrop
   Upon a stalk of green.

has latterly, while often using much the same manner, alternated his matter till nothing remains but some very rarefied joke:

Watching the unstoppable
Legs go by
With never a stumble
Between step and step.

Though my smile was broad
The legs could not see,
Though my laugh was loud
The legs could not hear.

My head dizzied then:
I wondered suddenly,
Might I too be a walker
From the knees down?

Gently I touched my shins.
The doubt unchained them:
They had run in twenty puddles
Before I regained them.

America has produced a series of 'hard-boiled', mocking poets from E. E. Cummings to Dorothy Parker and Stevie Smith. This poetry is usually strongly sentimental. It is the poetry of some one kicking against the pricks or shouting against the traffic. And the voice has an echo of the traffic in it.

But apart from short poems of escapist nonsense or tongue-in-the-cheek impressionism, no poets till recently wrote works of any length in the grand critical tradition of Pope or Byron. Recently, however, there have been two long poems of serious criticism in the lighter manner—'One-Way Song' by Wyndham Lewis and 'A Letter to Lord Byron' by Auden. Wyndham Lewis is not a professional poet and writes typically in an ostentatiously care-free manner. In 'One-Way Song' he is attacking the butts of his critical prose writings—the effeminacy and dilettantism of modern culture, the child-cult, the time-cult, the Lawrentian cult of the Blood. While considering Lewis's attitude unbalanced, sometimes inconsistent with his practice, and distorted by a kind of persecution mania, I think that in this long poem he presents many valuable critical ideas more forcibly than he does in prose—his manner here being a compromise between doggerel and grand satire. Witness his ironical criticism of the obscurantist doctrine of poetry I have discussed earlier in this book (exemplified in such poetry as is found in the periodical *Transition*):

Do not expect a work of the classic canon.
Take binoculars to these nests of camouflage—
Spy out what is *half-there*—the page-under-the-page.
Never demand the integral—never completion—
Always what is fragmentary—the promise, the presage—
Eavesdrop upon the soliloquy—stop calling the spade
    spade. . . .

and

And you'll hear a great deal more, where a sentence breaks in
    two,
Believe me, than ever the most certificated schoolmasters'
    darlings do!

When a clause breaks down (that's natural, for it's been prob-
     ably overtaxed)
Or the sense is observed to squint, or in a dashing grammatical
     tort,
You'll find more of the stuff of poetry than ever in stupid
     syntax!

I sabotage the sentence! With me is the naked word.
I spike the verb—all parts of speech are pushed over on their
     backs.
I am the master of all that is half-uttered and imperfectly
     heard.
Return with me where I am crying out with the gorilla and
     the bird.

Auden's 'Letter to Lord Byron' (1936) is a
tour de force, a challenge to the common statement
that to adopt an earlier poet's manner leads merely
to *pastiche*. In this long poem Auden uses an easy
Byronic stanza to convey a mass of contemporary
criticism, autobiography and gossip. The experiment succeeds. I doubt if he could have done
the same with heroic couplets modelled on Pope.
The heroic couplet is a specialized form adapted
to the leisurely Queen Anne world of Reason
and Propriety—a world which is no longer with
us. Byron's lighter stanzas, however, are a much
more elastic form, able to carry the discursive comments of a Don Juan on a world of flux and contradictions. Auden, who holds strongly that chat belongs
to poetry as well as incantation or lyrical statement, uses it easily and lucidly to give with point
and humour a memorable summary of his position:

A raw provincial, my good taste was tardy,
  And Edward Thomas I as yet preferred;
I was still listening to Thomas Hardy
  Putting divinity about a bird;
  But Eliot spoke the still unspoken word;
For gasworks and dried tubers I forsook
The clock at Grantchester, the English rook.

All youth's intolerant certainty was mine as
  I faced life in a double-breasted suit;
I bought and praised but did not read Aquinas,
  At the *Criterion*'s verdict I was mute,
  Though Arnold's I was ready to refute;
And through the quads dogmatic words rang clear,
'Good poetry is classic and austere'.

Auden in the last few years, in an attempt to do justice to the multiplicity of modern life, has tried many forms of light verse, taking hints from Skelton, from mummers' plays, from broadsheets, from American cowboy poetry, from nonsense verse, from jazz songs. Witness his Skeltonic polemic:

Heathcliffe before you as a newspaper peer:
I'm the sea-dog, he said, who shall steer this ship;
I advertise idiocy, uplift, and fear,
I succour the State, I shoot from the hip;
He grasped at God but God gave him the slip.
Life gave him one look and he lost his nerve,
So you'll get the thrashing you richly deserve.

Or his excellent Yeatsian fantasy which beneath its nonsense conceals a criticism of society:

And a hole in the bottom of heaven and Peter and Paul
And each smug surprised saint like parachutes to fall,
And every one-legged beggar to have no legs at all—

Cried the six cripples to the silent statue,
The six beggared cripples.

Or his ironic parody of jazz poetry:

He was my North, my South, and East and West,
My working week, and my Sunday rest;
My noon, my midnight, my talk, my song;
I thought that love could last for ever: I was wrong.

The stars are not wanted now, put out every one;
Pack up the moon and dismantle the sun;
Pour away the ocean, and sweep up the wood:
For nothing now can ever come to any good.

Lately, Auden has been writing light lyrics for music (a healthy occupation) and a series of straightforward, satirical contemporary ballads. These latter tend to be cheap, too facile, though Auden claims that they are full of sound observation. Thus 'The Ballad of Miss Gee', though amusing and very cleverly executed, has been rightly dismissed by Desmond MacCarthy as merely a piece of rather cruel spinster-baiting. He is better when he uses the ballad manner for a blend of sermon and fantasy, as in his 'Song for the New Year':

It's farewell to the drawing-room's civilized cry,
The professor's sensible whereto and why,
The frock-coated diplomat's social aplomb,
Now matters are settled with gas and with bomb.

I shall come, I shall punish, the Devil be dead:
I shall have caviare thick on my bread,
I shall build myself a cathedral for home
With a vacuum cleaner in every room.

I shall ride on the front in a platinum car,
My features shall shine, my name shall be Star:
Day long and night long the bells I shall peal,
And down the long street I shall turn the cartwheel.

Auden's various lighter manners have been copied by Day-Lewis but not successfully (see the satirical portions of 'The Magnetic Mountain' and the jazz experiments in 'A Time to Dance'). To use popular slang and buffoon-tricks successfully one must not use them purely in cold blood as a satirist or parodist; one must have some sympathy, to start with, with the popular world, the buffoon-world. Auden is by nature partly a buffoon, and largely a gossip; Day-Lewis is not.

Other younger poets, however, know how to employ the 'Grain of Salt' or the 'Urge to Nonsense'. Witness M'Diarmid's 'Prayer for a Second Flood', which shows the contemptuous high spirits of Burns:

There'd ha'e to be nae warnin'. Times ha'e changed
And Noahs are owre numerous nooadays,
(And them the vera folk to benefit maist!)
Knock the feet frae under them, O Lord, wha praise
Your unsearchable ways sae muckle and yet hope
    To keep within knowledgeable scope!

. . . .

Then flush the world in earnest. Let yoursel' gang,
Scour't to the bones, and mak' its marrow holes
Toom as a whistle as they used to be
In days I mind o' ere men fidged wi' souls,
But naething had forgotten you as yet
    Nor you forgotten it.

On a different plane, John Betjeman, a master of parody, presents through this form an accurate picture of those parts of modern England which are themselves parodies—neo-Gothic architecture, the odder sectarian religions, the Arts and Crafts movement, the suburbs. And William Plomer writes a mocking little ballad, 'The Murder on the Downs', on a newspaper theme:

> Past the inn and past the garage,
> Past the hypodermic steeple
> Ever ready to inject
> The opium of the people
>
> Under a sky without a cloud
> Lay the still unruffled sea,
> And in the bracken like a bed
> The murderee.

For poets to-day have to read the newspapers, and in a world where Mussolini, on the one hand, surpasses the wildest fantasies of Swift, and the English squire, on the other, hopes to retain his squirearchy and the lounge-lizard his lounge, the only reaction is often one of laughter.

ii

As light verse offers the poet a needed change from the intensity of the lyric, so drama offers him a change from the single voice. In the lyric the poet speaks with one voice only. In the drama he can do justice to the many different people within him.

Verse plays are in one respect truer to human nature than prose plays, in that they are rhythmical as human nature is rhythmical. A play is, from the start, a very artificial thing, so that naturalism on the stage tends to contradict its premisses. Why should people who live in rooms with only three walls talk just like you and me who live in four-walled rooms?

Poets during the nineteenth century wrote verse plays which were purely literary, unconditioned by contemporary life or the contemporary stage. Yeats, whose plays were produced in the Abbey Theatre at Dublin, has for all that not succeeded in shaking clear of literature. For he aimed, in his own words, at a 'distance from life'. This half-truth cleared the way for a more vital verse-drama, but Yeats was wrong in thinking that the form must be 'aristocratic', for he could not expect to have an 'aristocratic' audience. Hence his imitations of the Noh plays of Japan were still-born. But some of the limits which he imposed on himself were more fertile limits. Thus in an essay on 'The Tragic Theatre' (1910) he attacked the modern dramatist's obsession with character—'in mainly tragic art one distinguishes devices to exclude or lessen character'. Conversely, we may say that plays such as Tchehov's, which are best adapted to the portrayal of character, cannot perhaps attain to higher tragedy and that the man who wants to write tragedy is most likely to succeed in a verse-form or possibly in some form more like Expressionism.

The players and the action, for Yeats, are to be as strange and yet familiar as the people and actions in dreams. But the symbolism is to be implicit, concrete, not to be analysed—'Though I might discover what had been and might be again an abstract idea, no abstract idea must be present.' Here Yeats approaches Cocteau, who writes in a note on Orphée: 'Inutile de dire qu'il n'y a pas un seul symbole dans la pièce. Rien que du langage pauvre, du *poème agi*.'

But Yeats's earlier plays, written in verse throughout, are too much tapestry, too much flat charades. His later plays—such as *Resurrection*—are written in a rarefied prose interspersed with lyrics. He was driven to this compromise because his blank verse was not elastic enough to represent the changes of mood, the variations of tone, the dialectic of conflict, necessary to a play.

Most of the plays of the younger poets are also a mixture of verse and prose. The poetry consists in interpolations (such as the choruses in Auden and Isherwood's *The Dog Beneath the Skin*). This is unsatisfactory because one of the main reasons for verse drama is that verse unifies the drama. Spender's recent *Trial of a Judge* is a play written, on the Greek model, almost in verse throughout. But here the verse is so complex, so closely written, that, though readable, it almost fails to be hearable. Some form is required half-way between the healthy but vulgar hodge-podge of Auden and Isherwood and the arid dignity of Spender.

Poets' plays, so far, have hardly been successful as plays, but they have at least given opportunity for the writing of impressive didactic verse. Eliot's *Murder in the Cathedral* is nearly a play, but it is a foregone conclusion and a foregone conclusion is not dramatic. But it is good contemplative writing even though the attitude expressed may be unsympathetic to the more vital sections of the public. *The Ascent of F6* has a good dramatic theme and scores full marks from the psychologists, but is too much a puppet show and, besides, is written mainly in conversational prose with which the verse does not blend very happily.

Poets, however, should be encouraged to write dramatic verse as they should be encouraged to write narrative verse or occasional verse. It is particularly likely that they may find a good medium in radio plays. Also verse may be more suitable than prose for a commentary on certain types of films—witness Auden's verse commentary to the G.P.O. film, *Night Mail*. It is very good for the poet that he should employ certain forms which demand collaboration with other craftsmen. A poet should always be 'collaborating' with his public, but this public, in the mass, cannot make itself heard and he has to guess at its requirements and its criticisms. But what it requires will be largely what he requires himself, so that the poet is likely to find bits of himself in the film-studio or on the stage which he would never notice among the books and papers in his study.

XI

CONCLUSION

WRITING about poetry often becomes a parlour game. The critic is more interested in producing a water-tight system of criticism than in the objects which are his data. I have written this book as one who enjoys reading and writing certain (probably limited) kinds of poetry and is only concerned with criticism in so far as it clears away misapprehensions and opens the gate to poetry itself.

I consider that the poet is a blend of the entertainer and the critic or informer; he is not a legislator, however unacknowledged, nor yet, essentially, a prophet. As informer, he is not a photographic or scientific informer, but more like the 'informer', in the derogatory sense—he is grinding an axe or showing off, telling tales about his enemies, flattering his friends. His object is not merely to record a fact but to record a fact *plus and therefore modified by* his own emotional reaction to it; this involves mannerism in its presentation—hence the tricks of poetry. Poetic truth therefore is distinct from scientific truth. The poet does not give you a full and accurate picture of the world nor a full and accurate picture of himself, but he gives you an amalgam which, if successful, represents truthfully his own relation to the world. This is a valuable function, for we are all concerned with our relations to our worlds, and the odds

are that we have much in common with the poet and
our world with his.

My own prejudice, therefore, is in favour of poets
whose worlds are not too esoteric. I would have a poet
able-bodied, fond of talking, a reader of the newspapers, capable of pity and laughter, informed in
economics, appreciative of women, involved in personal relationships, actively interested in politics,
susceptible to physical impressions. The relationship
between life and literature is almost impossible to
analyse, but it should not be degraded into something
like the translation of one language into another.
For life is not literary, while literature is not, in spite
of Plato, essentially second hand.

I have already said that the ordinary man is always
using language poetically, but I would maintain that
ordinary conversation itself is something distinct in
kind from those facts—even if they are moods and
emotions—which it attempts to represent. Communication is a utility, but it is also a luxury even as
the development of species is, on analysis, a luxury.
This is why I do not think, with Stephen Spender,
that 'poetic *statement*' is the whole story, for what the
poet states is *partly* something new. I can never, as
most philosophers would admit, state an object *x* or
an event *x*; I can only make a statement about that
object or event. Therefore, if the statement is to be
worth making, it must have something to it which
·the object or event had not. Suppose I am in love:
that is an event. Now if I make even the barest
statement about that, if I say merely 'I am in love',
this statement is something more (though also some-

thing less) than the event, for it is a judgement and no event is a judgement. Now why do I make a judgement in words about something which I have already experienced as event? Because I find the judgement complementary to the event, and, being human, I find event plus judgement more satisfactory than pure event. A twist in human nature, not found in lower animals, makes people look to thoughts for the vindication of their experiences. And with our thoughts go words. But once we are among words, words have a life of their own (though governed by their heredity from experience). In order to keep a correspondence between our words and the original facts, we have to let the words act those facts on their own stage and in their own peculiar way. Nijinsky, just before he went mad, got up to give a dance, saying: 'I am going to dance the War.' It would be no good saying to such an artist, 'You cannot dance a war, you can only fight it.' In the same way the poet dances his experiences in words.

Subject is automatically formalized when it is put into any sort of words. It is impossible to write either without form or without subject. But subject can to some extent swamp form or form invalidate subject. It is the ratio between the two which makes a good poem. Subject must work itself out in pattern but not be emasculated by pattern. In this book I have tried to show how modern poetry has set out to readjust the ratio, which had been upset by various conflicting extremisms.

The question of expression implies a radical distinction between disguise and dress. Thoughts must be dressed in words as soul must be dressed in body. And obviously a thought or rather the complex of thought-and-emotion, is often so intricate that its dress must be subtly cut so as not to obscure its curves. Wordsworth's 'Lucy' poems are magnificently simple, but such simplicity could not be made the rule. The poet can sometimes be direct where the ordinary man is evasive, but sometimes he must look on all sides where the ordinary man only looks ahead. I have argued that the younger poets to-day are becoming more direct, focusing their aim on some ideal from the practical world which is also the ideal of many ordinary men. But such poets will still tend to look about them, to qualify, to put in the shadows. Witness the disapproval among official Communists aroused by Spender's *Trial of a Judge*.

The poet must not completely surrender control of his poem—or his poem's control of itself. My objection to surrealism applies equally to pure propaganda-verse. In Russia shortly after the revolution the communist poet, Maiakovski, established a 'word workshop' which was ready to supply all revolutionaries with 'any quantity of poetry desired'; and the poetry he would give them would be exactly the poetry they asked for. But poetry, if it does this, defeats its own end. Poetry, either as entertainment or criticism, is only valuable if it can add something to the experience of its public, this addition often consisting merely in the illumination of that public's own experience. An advertisement is not expected to be true, but there might be an argument for the poet's advertising himself. If, however, he is only asked to advertise to the public the goods which they already possess and are thoroughly familiar with and have no need to buy from any one else, the poet's function is superfluous.

The distinction must always be maintained between belief and propaganda. It is nonsense to say, as many say nowadays, that all great poetry has in all periods been essentially propaganda. The propagandist is consciously and solely concerned with converting people to a cause or creed. If Homer, Virgil, Shakespeare, or Milton meant to do this, they were thoroughly bad propagandists. Milton may have converted people to Puritan Christianity but only by the way. He would have written his poems very differently if that had been his sole object. The fact that a poem in which a belief is implicit may convert some whom direct propaganda does not touch, far from proving that that poem is propaganda, only proves that propaganda *can* be beaten on its own ground by something other than itself, so that we can admit that poetry can incidentally have effects like those of propaganda though its proper function is not propagandist.

I have already maintained that major poetry usually implies a belief. Therefore the fact that beliefs are increasing among poets should conduce to a wider, more fertile, and possibly a major poetry. But, *for the poet*, any belief, any creed (and beliefs and creeds tend to be *a priori*) should be compromised with his own individual observation. (Men of action in certain circumstances may benefit through being unobservant

or uncritical, but if the poet is to be required to do
this he may as well give up writing and merely act.
I do not deny that at a certain moment of history
this might be the poet's duty—but as a man, not as a
poet.) Shelley was an inferior poet because he did
not qualify his dogmas with observation.

This can be seen not only in Shelley's political
poetry, which divorces principles from particulars,
but in Shelley's constant implication that pure poetry
divorces universal beauty from the particulars which
it 'informs' (Shelley being a Platonist with a bias in
favour of the Forms as *transcendent*—a point never
quite made clear by Plato himself):

> On a poet's lips I slept
> Dreaming like a love-adept
> In the sound his breathing kept;
> Nor seeks nor finds he mortal blisses,
> But feeds on the aerial kisses
> Of shapes that haunt thought's wildernesses.
> He will watch from dawn to gloom
> The lake-reflected sun illume
> The yellow bees in the ivy-bloom,
>   *Nor heed nor see what things they be;* [italics mine]
> But from these create he can
> Forms more real than living man,
>   Nurslings of immortality!

Enthusiasm such as Shelley's is a great asset to a
poet, but is the better if tempered with Reason and
observation of fact. We have seen that among modern
poets Eliot lacked enthusiasm while Lawrence lacked
reason or any reasoned system. Lawrence preaches
anarchy:

Yet, O my young man, there is a vivifier.
There is that which makes us eager.
While we are eager, we think nothing of it.
Sum ergo non cogito.
But when our eagerness leaves us, we are godless and full of
    thought.

On these premisses it was inconsistent in Lawrence
to *write*. For what he wanted, or said he wanted, was
to stay in the pure event and never stray towards
judgement.

Auden, as I have pointed out, made use of the
Lawrentian (or Whitmanesque) 'urge' by canalizing
it. He reintroduced the deliberating will, Aristotle's
proairesis. Thus in his poem on Spain the stricken
nations are represented as appealing to the life-
principle (the automatic impulse of Nature so prized
by Whitman and Lawrence):

And the nations combine each cry, invoking the life
That shapes the individual belly. . . .

And the life, if it answers at all, replies from the heart
And the eyes and the lungs, from the shops and squares of the
        city:
    'O no, I am not the mover;
Not to-day; not to you. To you, I'm the

Yes-man, the bar-companion, the easily duped;
I am whatever you do. I am your vow to be
    Good, your humorous story.
I am your business voice. I am your marriage.

What's your proposal? To build the just city? I will.
I agree. Or is it the suicide pact, the romantic
    Death? Very well, I accept, for
I am your choice, your decision. Yes, I am Spain.'

Lawrence would have left it to 'the life' to make his decision. Auden, though brought up on Homer Lane to recognize the importance of 'the life', believes in canalizing it in certain directions approved by the mind.

Edward Upward, in an article in *The Mind in Chains*, maintained that no writer now can write well unless he is an active member of the workers' movement. This is an overstatement (to be expected in a writer who had taken to the workers' movement as an escape from escapist fantasy). There is no reason why even a fascist should not nowadays write a good love-song or a good nonsense poem or epigram. But it is probably true that, for the production nowadays of major literature or of literature on a large scale, a sympathy is required in the writer with those forces which at the moment make for progress. The important events outside him must penetrate him in the same way as Euripides was penetrated by the Peloponnesian War or by the intellectual discoveries of the sophists.

Poets like Auden, Spender, and Day Lewis have adopted a system of belief which they have not yet quite grown into. But on the whole they do not state such beliefs more explicitly than is warranted by their natural emotional reaction to them. Only Day Lewis's sermonizing appears sometimes too *voulu* (commensurately with his technique). One grows into a belief more quickly, and more solidly, in a crisis and a crisis might make these poets better or produce other and better poets. But in the meantime it is desirable that poets like these should write honestly, their poetry keeping pace with their lives and with their beliefs as affecting their lives, neither lagging behind in an obsolete romanticism nor running ahead to an assurance too good to be true. When the crisis comes, poetry may for the time be degraded or even silenced, but it will reappear, as one of the chief embodiments of human dignity, when people once more have time for play and criticism.